FROM PRISON TO PURPOSE

A Journey to Answering Life's Greatest Question

Donna,
God Bless
you and your
Purpose!
Steve

STEVE HOPPER

From Prison to Purpose

ISBN:1503005380
ISBN 13: 9781503005389
Library of Congress Control Number: 2014919242
CreateSpace Independent Publishing Platform
North Charleston, South Carolina

DEDICATION

I dedicate this book to my loving wife and mother of our children, Lauren. Thank you for loving me through thick and thin and for always being my biggest supporter and my rock. To be able to share this life with you is truly a gift from God.

I dedicate this to my mom, Shirley. Thank you for giving me life, and for always loving me unconditionally. You were the first and best example of God's love I ever witnessed.

I dedicate this to my dad, Larry, who is in heaven. Thank you for giving me life. I miss you, and I hope I make you proud.

I dedicate this to my four awesome children, Chloe, Cory, Katie, and Cody. You bring a purpose to my life, and you light up my world.

I dedicate this to my brothers from other mothers, Marks, Bill, Mikey, Sean, and my uncle Stan. Thank you for always believing in me, and for always having my back.

And I dedicate this book to my sister Stephanie and to the rest of my family and friends who have encouraged me along the way. Especially to my granddaddy, who gave me the piece of advice that changed my life.

Contents

Foreword

I remember it as if it was yesterday...*"I'm sorry, but you've been laid off."* I pinched myself because in my eight years of engineering I had escaped layoffs and downsizing. *What is happening?* I thought. The response was a calming peace that came over me. When it was all over, I had been laid off on my birthday, but deep down inside, I knew that this wasn't something bad; it was actually something good. It felt like God was sending me a message: *"Happy birthday, Daughter! I have something better and exciting for you!"* Since that day the journey to fulfill my life purpose has been an exciting roller-coaster ride!

As a transformation speaker and coach, I meet men and women from different cultures and backgrounds around the world who are asking the same question, one way or another: "What is my purpose in life?" I find joy in fulfilling my purpose by supporting them in the transformation from being who they are now to becoming who they were created to be.

Within the pages of *From Prison to Purpose,* you will begin to unravel your answer to that question. If you have ever wondered if you even have a purpose, then this book will quiet those wonderings. If you are currently in a situation where you are feeling drained, stressed, or frustrated, it could be that you are not being true to yourself in being who you were created to be, and this book will give you the courage you need to be still and listen to the divine nudges within.

You have a purpose that you were created to fulfill. God, our creator, designed you with the right personality, the correct skills and abilities, the most moving desire, and the most foundational strengths, uniquely designed and packaged for you and your purpose. Your likes and dislikes are not a coincidence; they are for a purpose. God uses even the mistakes, mishaps, challenges, and tragedies to provide you wisdom and develop the strengths that you need along your journey.

The fulfillment that you experience when you finally decide to take that step of faith and begin to take that journey to pursue and fulfill your purpose is one that will take you from existing and surviving to living and thriving.

You are going to be so glad that you chose to read this book. Get ready for a change that will quiet your doubts and empower your pursuits. In this book, you'll soon discover that your purpose is not a moment or a destination, but that it actually fuels you in the journey we call life.

Join Steve Hopper as he opens his heart and shares his journey from prison to his purpose, and you'll begin to see page by page, chapter by chapter, that yes, you have a purpose and that God has been waiting to take that journey with you all along.

Enjoy the journey!

—Clestine, the Purpose Coach
Author of *Knuggets of Knowledge to Get Unstuck*
Founder of www.DivineDiscipline.com

Endorsements

"From Prison to Purpose is a great read. I could relate on so many levels of Steve's story, I even found myself crying in one part of the book. At the end I actually thanked Jesus for answering the question I asked Him many years ago, that same question Steve urges us all to ask, "What's my purpose?". In the grand scheme of things I am honored to have had a small role in helping Steve find his true purpose and grateful to see him lead so many young men and women to Christ. Well done Steve!"

Chris Cherp - Overflow Magazine

"Steve Hopper has written a powerful book of how he turned a setback into a comeback in the Biggest game of all... Life! He shares who the Real CHAMPION is and provides a clear picture of a Worldly Quest vs. A Quest for REAL AND TRUE SUCCESS!"

-Tyrone Keys
World Champion Chicago Bears
Founder of All Pro Community

"Powerful and transformational, this book will inspire and equip you to find your purpose in life!"

-Pastor Joe Jackson
Savanna Church

Introduction

"What should I do with my life?" This is a powerful question that most of us ask ourselves at one point or another. Or even the more important question..."What is my life's purpose?" Sometimes we wonder if there really is a purpose for our lives. And if there is, how do we go about figuring it out? These are all questions that I have asked over the course of my life. In the darkest moments of my life, these questions have haunted me.

I have heard people say things like "The meaning of life is to live a life of meaning." Cool, but what does that mean? They even say things like "Until you discover the purpose of your life, you are living a life of mediocrity." And I would read quotes like "Rise and be great, and do the great things you were meant to do. Look deep inside you and realize what your life's purpose is and embrace it." Great, I'm in...but how do I come to realize my purpose? For most people this is a very difficult question to answer.

In our humanistic culture, people pursue many things, thinking that in them they will find meaning. Some of these pursuits include business success, wealth, good relationships, sex, entertainment, and doing good to others. People have testified that while they have achieved their goals of wealth, good relationships, and pleasure, there was still a deep void inside them, a feeling of emptiness that nothing seemed to fill.

In *From Prison to Purpose*, we will explore that emptiness and all that comes with it. I will take you on the journey that I took to realize my destiny in life. Here I will share with you the blueprint God laid out for me in order to find and understand the answer to life's greatest question. This is a story of tears and triumph, success and failure, and the battle that rages on for our lives. My hope in sharing this message with you is that you, too, will start to ask that all-important purpose question and, in doing so, come to realize the answer for yourself. It's an answer that carries eternal significance.

Let the journey to answering life's greatest question begin...

Chapter 1

FAINT LIGHT

Faint Light

It was cold and dark...I crouched down in the corner of the room and pulled my knees tightly to my chest. As I heard the yells and screams around me, I almost felt a sense of security in that cell. Through the darkness I observed my surroundings. The walls were solid concrete, like a prison inside of a prison. The single bed made of steel and bolted to the wall was a far cry from the bed I had left behind. There was a toilet placed against the opposite wall, also made of cold steel, and nothing in the room gave the slightest sign of comfort. That was it...Wait, I take that back. There hung a sense of failure and loneliness there that weighed down on me like a ton of bricks. And at times I felt as though the walls were closing in on me.

It was 9:00 p.m., lights-out time, and I couldn't help thinking back to the lights-out time from my childhood. My mom would come in my room and pull the covers up tightly around me and kiss me good night, and shortly after, my dad would pop his head in and say, "Good night, champ," before turning off the lights. But as that large steel door slammed shut to seal me in for the night, my fond image of the past was stripped immediately from my mind. The darkness surrounded me; it was so dark that I could not see a foot in front of my face. I was in a whole different world now, and it was nothing like the world I had left behind.

Thoughts of the past gave me comfort in the darkness. However, I knew I needed to get those thoughts out of my mind, because as much as they comforted me, they tormented me just the same. I had so many positive things going for me prior to that moment. The thoughts of all I had lost and all I had left behind caused me to drop my head and cry. I rested my head on my knees, and the tears began to flow uncontrollably.

In the darkness of my cell, I was alone with just my thoughts. I thought of a life that was no more, and I thought of a life moving forward that I was scared to death of. *How am I ever going to survive this?* I thought. *Will I be forgotten by my friends and family, who have always been there for me?* After all, I was only one year into a ten-year sentence, and ten years seemed like a long time to a seventeen-year-old kid. For me at that time, it felt like an eternity that would never end.

There was a dark force hovering over that place like a black cloud that crushed dreams and suffocated all hope. Just in the short time I had been there, I had already seen so many horrible things. I'd experienced humility, fear, and an evil force that I had not been exposed to previously in my life. I felt it from the very first moment I arrived.

Nothing my parents taught me in life had prepared me for what I was experiencing at that time. Nothing taught by my teachers, coaches, or anyone for that matter had prepared me for the environment that I was in now. At that point, I had already fought for my life on many occasions, and I had already witnessed others lose their lives to that violent place. Every waking moment was a struggle and a battle to survive. Each day when I walked out of that cell, I wondered if it would be my last.

I stayed crouched down in the corner, and I thought back to my first week there. During that first week, I met a guy they called "Slim." Slim was from the same hometown as me, and even though Slim and I had not known each other on the outside, because we were from the same place, we bonded immediately. Slim had already been there for a while, and he quickly taught me a few things that would keep me from getting myself killed. Slim taught me things like the specific times that were safe for taking showers. For example, four times a day, the guards came around and counted the inmates to make sure none had escaped. Each of the four count times took place at the same time every day, and inmates would be on their best behavior during these times because they knew the guards would be making their rounds. If there really was a safe time to take a shower, one of those times would be it.

Slim also taught me one day in the chow hall that your spoon could double as a mirror. If you held your spoon just the right way, the backside of your spoon would act as a mirror and show you the things that were taking place behind you. This way you could see if someone was coming up to stab you from behind while you ate your meal. Slim also shared with me the places on the compound that were safe to venture to and the places that were not. Over the first few weeks, he showed me the ins and the outs and the dos and the don'ts of prison life. Above all, Slim taught me that the normal rules of the outside world simply did not apply any longer. When you're in prison, you're living on a different planet, where all that matters to you is surviving the experience with as little damage as possible.

Never in a million years, would I have imagined that this would be my life. The world I had left was so much different than the one I was in. My life was as dark and gloomy as the cell that I sat in. On the inside, I had no real friends, no family, and no one I could truly trust, not even Slim. Most of my life, I had been surrounded by people who loved and supported me. I had people in my life who were always there to give an encouraging word in times of despair. But in prison, compassion and kindness were considered weaknesses, and weakness was not something you wanted to show to others. I was all alone, and I depended on the memories of the people back home to give me strength.

I pulled my knees even tighter to my chest, and I drifted off into memory land. I reminisced about my childhood, my family, and my friends. I thought of the many good times my friends and I had shared over the years. I was reminded of past loves, and I thought about love lost as I sat there in the darkness. I thought about my sister and how I wished I would have been a better brother to her. I wept heavily as I pictured the pain on my mother's face as she watched me take my fall. And then there was my father. He and I had bumped heads so many times over the past several years leading up to that moment. My dad and I had never seen eye to eye, and our relationship had gone through some serious rough patches along the way.

I wondered what they were doing at that exact moment. Were they thinking of me, and did they miss me as deeply as I missed them? Surely they must have, because I had not been gone that long. My family had done an amazing job of being there to support me, but many of my friends had already disappeared. I remember questioning why the friends I spent so much time with growing up had abandoned me. Was it because I was out of sight that I became out of mind also? In the loneliness and darkness of that cell, I wasn't sure about anything, and I questioned everything.

So many different emotions came upon me as I sat there in the darkness. I thought about all of the stories I had heard about people losing their minds in prison, and I knew I had already met a few of them. As sad as it was, I could totally see how it could happen. I stayed crouched down in the corner of that cell, alone with my thoughts, my fears, and my heartache. It was a heartache that was almost unbearable, and I really began to question if I would have the strength to go on. I questioned whether or not I would have the strength to endure this emotional turmoil for the entire ten years of my sentence. Again, I wondered how I was ever going to survive. I was scared to death, and I felt a sense of hopelessness that I had never felt before.

If there was a light at the end of that tunnel, I couldn't see it through the darkness. The weight of the world felt as though it were crushing me. The fear, regret, and hopelessness that I felt were almost suffocating. As I sat there in the loneliness of that cell, I even contemplated taking my own life and ending it all. As tempting as it was at the time, suicide was not an option. *I could not imagine the impact that decision would have on my family*, I thought. But I knew I couldn't go on like this if I were going to survive the hell I was in, both physically and mentally; something would have to change. I needed to figure out a way to overcome this place and not let it consume me if I were going to make it out alive. But I had no idea where to start. I was in the darkest moment of my life, my back was against the wall, and I didn't feel like I had any way out.

My eyes flooding with tears, I raised my head from its resting place upon my knees to see a faint light penetrating beneath the door of the prison cell. And what happened next would change my life forever...

Chapter 2

The Backstory

The Backstory

Before I tell you what happened that fateful night in the darkness, I have to tell you what led me to that place and to the moment that would change everything in my life. Life is a journey full of choices shaping both our success and our failure. Let me tell you where I began my journey full of tears and triumphs, choices and consequences, and the lessons lying within—lessons that could reveal the answer to life's greatest question.

Some people have experienced life-altering events or situations in their childhood. I really didn't have any of those. I grew up in a typical middle-class family, and both my dad and my mom worked hard to make ends meet. My father worked as an operations manager for a large freight line company, and my mother bounced between being a stay-at-home mom and working various jobs in the health care field. I came from a loving family, and my parents always did their best to provide for my sister and me. I remember my father had one of those very demanding corporate jobs and worked a lot of hours. But financially, we did not want for much.

My mother was the spiritual leader of the house and the glue that held it all together. On Sundays, she would drag my sister and me to church, even when we did not want to go. My father would attend every once in a while when he wasn't too tired from a hectic workweek. My mom was a people person, the type of person who never meets a stranger. She was friendly, outgoing, and compassionate. She had a heart of gold, and everyone could see it from the very first moment they met her. Her smile alone could light up a room. I was definitely a mama's boy growing up.

My mother and I still have a special relationship. She is always the person who lifts me up with words of encouragement and praise. No matter what I am going through in life, the good, the bad, and the ugly, she is there. She can always tell when something is wrong just by the look on my face. My mom is the kind of person who puts everyone else's needs above her own, and I learned a lot from her growing up. I learned compassion and forgiveness, and I learned how to unconditionally love other people. No matter where life has led us or what we have each faced in our lives, our family and our well-being have always been my mother's main focus.

My dad was a very charismatic person and the life of the party. He was always cracking jokes and making everyone laugh. But he had a very serious side to him as well. He was a professional and a natural-born salesman. Like my mom, he, too, had a heart of gold and the best intentions in everything he did. As my father excelled in his career, with every new promotion came a move. For the first ten years of my life, we were transferred up and down the southeastern United States. These transfers happened about every two years.

In 1991, my dad made one last transfer to Tampa, Florida. He knew all of the transferring was making it hard for the family to get settled into any one place, so he told his company that Tampa would be his final move. As I look back now, I realize what an important role those moves play in my life today. Every few years, I went to a new state and a new school, and each time I faced the task of making new friends. I'm thankful for those times today as I see how they taught me at a young age to develop relationships in any circumstances.

Most of my life, I watched my father be a slave to his job. I remember as a kid there being many events he was unable to attend because of his work schedule. Being a salaried employee in an upper-management position enabled the company to pimp him out whenever they needed to. He worked nights, days, and weekends—all the time, it seemed. He worked hard and made ends meet, but his work schedule definitely took its toll on our homelife and his relationship with me.

When I reached my teenage years, my dad and I had many struggles. As I look back now, I realize he and I were so much alike that bumping heads with each other was inevitable. My dad was an excellent provider, and even though the ends were met and we did not want for much, my parents were still just surviving. Today as I observe my surroundings, I see so many people who are much like my parents were back then—just going through life at ninety miles an hour, working and trying to survive. Most people don't slow down long enough to enjoy the life they are living, and they never slow down long enough to question if there is something more to life.

Even with their busy schedules, my parents still managed to instill in me the foundation needed to be successful in life. The morals, ethics, support, and encouragement I needed to succeed were all present.

At this point in my life growing up, I just enjoyed being a kid. I did most of the things a normal kid would do. I fought with my older sister, and I did little mischievous acts to get attention. I played outside with my friends, I enjoyed going to school, and I flirted with all the little girls in my class—pretty normal stuff. I was involved at one point in almost every sport available. I played basketball, baseball, football, wrestling, and so on. Sports were such a big part of my childhood. I look back at those times now, and I realize the character lessons I received from playing sports. Being part of a team and having a coach pour lessons of discipline and commitment into me was a big plus.

I recommend all parents out there make sure their children are involved in some sport or character-building activity. The lessons learned will play a major role in the children's lives. Winning and losing are things we all experience in life, and the sooner in life we learn how to handle both, the better off we are.

Out of all of the sports that I played growing up, football was, by far, my favorite. I started playing football at the age of four years old, and all I knew at that point was that if I ran around and crashed into everyone who got in my way, then eventually I would get the guy who had the ball. That was my theory and my approach, and it worked! As time went on, however, I grew up and developed some real technique. I still miss playing football to this day—running around aimlessly just crashing into people. No matter what town we were residing in when I was growing up, one of the first things my parents did was track down the best football league in town. They did everything they could to support my passion for the sport.

Settling down in Tampa in 1991 was exciting for the family. My parents chose a great suburban neighborhood close to the neighborhood where my dad's brother Stan lived. We were now within walking distance to family, which was something that we had never had before. The junior high and high school were within walking distance, also, and both schools had great football programs. Everyone seemed to be thrilled about the move.

Everyone was happy, except for my sister. Stephanie was a senior in high school at the time, and she was pretty settled back in North Carolina, where we had lived before. She was on the cheerleading team at her school and had a great network of close friends there, and of course, she had a boyfriend. The move was very hard on her, to say the least.

Starting over in Tampa in the middle of her senior year became more than she could handle. And soon, the strain of a long-distance relationship with her boyfriend took its toll. Ultimately the relationship ended, sending my sister into a deep state of depression. This became a difficult time for our family.

My dad was working long hours getting settled into his new facility, and Mom was focused on getting life in order there in Tampa. I stayed busy and preoccupied getting acclimated and making new friends of my own. I can't help thinking that the rest of us were so preoccupied with our own lives that we didn't even notice the struggle Stephanie was going through. Her depression continued to progress to thoughts of suicide, all of which she kept to herself.

Somehow the school got wind of my sister's threats against her own life, and they called the state. My parents were notified that the state was going to take over custody of my sister and hospitalize her. When the state takes over, the family loses all control in most situations. And unfortunately, this was the case for my parents. My sister was depressed and looking for attention, and I don't believe she ever had any intentions of doing any harm to herself. But regardless, the system had been notified, and she belonged to them now. This devastated my parents, and my sister as well. I remember going to visit her and seeing her beg and plead to come home as I watched my mom cry, knowing that her hands were tied.

We always had an environment at home that was open and understanding. There had really been no major drama to speak of prior to this time in our lives. I watched my parents as they struggled to deal with what was happening. I received bits and pieces of information along the way, but I was on a need-to-know basis concerning the details surrounding my sister. Because I wasn't privy to the seriousness of what was happening with her, I went on with my days as if nothing was wrong. I was too young and immature to truly understand what my family was going through at that time.

My parents stood by my sister, and with many prayers, she eventually returned home and moved on with her life. The situation wasn't easy for anyone involved, and we did not recover overnight. The state had kept her for weeks, and this event took its toll emotionally on my family. I can see now how God used that situation to strengthen my parents and my sister. They were going to need that strength, because what I would put them through a few years later would require all of the strength they could possess.

A few months after all of the drama, life got back to normal, and I remained fully engaged in my own understanding of life. The next few years were full of exciting new experiences as I started my high school years. Throughout that time, I continued to feed my love for football, and I became one of only a few sophomores to make the varsity team at my school. I was still on track to fulfilling my dream of playing college football one day. My junior year I began to get some attention from local colleges, and I developed hopes of one day becoming a Florida Gator. But before my childhood dream could manifest, things started to change.

Like always when we moved to a new place, I had established a pretty solid network of friends. One friend in particular even grew to become like a brother to me. Marks and I met in the eighth grade at the beginning of football season, and we quickly became best friends, who were almost inseparable. Marks played fullback, and man, was he good. He was one guy I didn't want to meet in the middle of the field. Short and stocky, he was as solid as a rock. Over the next few years, Marks and I stayed very close and enjoyed together the success we were both having on the field. Both of our futures looked bright at the time, but as the years progressed, we both faced some major challenges together.

Those challenges would come later, however. At the moment, the only challenge I faced was staying focused. I was doing a great job until one day a cute blond-haired, blue-eyed girl in my homeroom class caught my eye. Shortly after, in the midst of teenage hormones flying, I caught her eye as well. With mutual feelings being obvious, we began to court. During this courtship I experienced feelings I had never felt before. They were feelings that, looking back, I was too immature to handle properly.

Our courtship and my feelings for her soon took my focus completely away from what I truly wanted to do with my life. Puppy love consumed my every thought. I became unfocused on my schoolwork and on playing football. However, I still maintained both, but not with the passion I had before. This courtship lasted through most of my high school years. But due to the immaturity surrounding it, our relationship eventually came to an end, and I took it very hard. She was, in fact, my first love and also my first heartbreak—a heartbreak that sent me into a state of confusion emotionally.

She had become such a part of my everyday thoughts and activities. *What do I do?* I wondered. I tried to refocus on my schoolwork and my passion for football. I continued to play ball, but the dedication and discipline I had once had in the past went by the wayside and allowed new influences to come into my life.

"'Their hearts are always going astray, and they have not known my ways'" (Heb. 3:10).

Around this time my best buddy Marks suffered a knee injury that ended his football career. And without football Marks became vulnerable to negative influences as well. Marks and I had always done everything together, and both of us having our heads in the gutter at the same time became a recipe for disaster.

I quickly became a person with no drive and no focus, and I was lost. Just living moment to moment, I never stopped and asked myself the question "Where is my life headed?" I was only concerned with living in the moment, and that moment quickly became a distraction from all that I had wanted to do with my life. There was a buildup of events that led to that seemingly fateful night later on, a night where a split-second decision changed everything—a night that changed the course of my life forever. With my dreams still somewhat intact but not focused on them, I gave into emotion. I made decisions that did not support the morals and beliefs I'd been taught all of my life.

With my best buddy and partner in crime Marks by my side, I began to engage in a lot of negative activities. I found myself partying and drinking way too often, chasing girls, and even sampling drugs. At the time, I had a promising future in front of me, with everything I had dreamed of as a child within reach. If I stayed focused, I had an opportunity to go and play college football. So why was I acting this way? Why the sudden shift in gears? Why would I let those dreams slip away? I was caught up in the moment...I was having fun, and no one could tell me differently.

This is when things between my father and me began to really escalate. Our relationship over the years had always been volatile, but my new attitude took things to another level. My dad was really struggling with the choices I was making in my life at the time. He had always been a strict disciplinarian; it was something he had learned from his father.

Throughout my teen years, I rejected my father's style of parenting. I believe my father was at a loss on how to deal with the fact that I was about to flush my dreams and future down the toilet. He was still working long hours at the time and was hardly around. When he was there, he was stepping down on me for the decisions I was making. I was not at all receptive to his attempts at guidance. In fact, they had the complete opposite effect. My insubordination and his frustration collided on more than one occasion. I was too big to spank, and if he restricted me, I would just leave. Our inability to communicate with each other even led to fistfights on several occasions.

How did we get to that point? Was it my father's strict disciplinary style that I rejected? Was it the fact that his career had caused him to be detached for so long? Or was it the chip on my shoulder and my new attitude that was causing all of the problems at home? I believe it was a combination of all of the above, and the end result was me leaving my house and breaking my poor mother's heart in the process.

Marks had been dealing with very similar struggles at home with his mom. How convenient—my partner in crime was headed down the same path as me. Marks's family were witnessing his poor decisions and calling him out on them as well. As a result, Marks, too, decided he would be better off outside of his home. So there we were, two friends who, just a short time ago, had our whole futures ahead of us. We had the bull by the horns and the world at our fingertips. In such a short period of time, however, all of that had changed. Now by our own choice, we were fending for ourselves. This book would be too long if I tried to tell you all the things Marks and I got into during this time on our own. Let's just say we were both headed together in the wrong direction.

And soon it would all come to an abrupt end.

Chapter 3

The Fall

THE FALL

EVERY FRIDAY NIGHT my friends and I would meet at the local McDonald's parking lot. From there we would socialize and get information as to where the weekend's parties were taking place. Once enough people were in agreement as to where to go, a caravan of cars would head out. Sometimes hundreds of high school kids headed out to drink at a house, or maybe even at a field party. Every weekend we would create a disaster waiting to happen. We were kids behind the wheel, drinking, partying, and getting into whatever seemed fun at the time. I can't believe there were not more incidences to speak of surrounding these weekends. It's amazing that any of us made it out of high school alive.

One particular Friday night, another teenager and I became examples of what happens when immaturity and irresponsibility meet on the same field. This particular Friday my friends and I were presented with a choice to attend a party locally, where we would be among friends, or to attend a party some distance away, where we would be partying with a bunch of people from our rival high school. Feeling adventurous that night, we decided to take the drive to the second party. Most of our friends stayed behind. They thought we were crazy to attend the other party, and those friends proved to be right.

A handful of us headed out, the night destined from the very beginning to end badly. After what seemed like a long drive, we arrived at a secluded private beach hidden on the outskirts of Tampa Bay. As we pulled up, we noticed the immense bonfire surrounded by what had to be a few hundred teenagers partying. It seemed harmless and looked like fun, so we made our way down to the beach. Unfortunately, we soon realized we were the outsiders at this party, and we were not welcome.

We mingled for a few minutes, and then it happened. The alcohol and the atmosphere together were the perfect combination needed for trouble to take place. An argument erupted between one of my friends and another guy at the party. Before I knew what was happening, a fight broke out. In a matter of moments, it was complete chaos. Another friend of mine engaged, and I soon found myself rushing into the mess as well. During the altercation, I hit another teenager and delivered a blow in that split second that had an impact on many lives forever. The swift blow to his temple caused any hopes and dreams that either of us had to fall by the wayside.

I retrieved Marks, and we fled to our cars before the fight could get any worse. At the time I did not know the severity of my choice. At the time I didn't think anything of the altercation. We had been there before. We had been in fights before; it was like any other Friday night, or so I thought. In that moment I was oblivious to the consequences the choice that night would have.

A few days later, two sheriff's deputies showed up at my parents' doorstep with a warrant for my arrest. The other teen I hit during the brawl on Friday night had slipped into a coma. The warrant the sheriff provided was for the charge of attempted murder. In that moment everything in my life changed forever. All my hopes and dreams, all I thought I was going to do with my life, had died on the beach that Friday night.

But wait, how could this be? I questioned. I hadn't tried to kill anyone. It was just a fight. How could this have happened? How could things in my life have gotten so screwed up so quickly? I was not at home when the deputy delivered the warrant, and my father was the one to receive the news first. Because I had been charged with attempted murder, the police issued a statement that I was considered to be "armed and extremely dangerous." Because of this, my parents were in fear for my safety. My father picked me up to turn me in in an attempt to avoid any misguided judgment by the police.

I still remember the car ride to the county jail that day and the conversation that my dad and I had on the way there. We had definitely had our struggles with each other. But he was there, he said, and he was going to stand by me through thick and thin. I could almost hear his heart breaking, knowing that he was going to have to hand his only son over to the authorities. My dad and I had had a rough go leading up to that car ride. But we were family—he was my dad, and I was his son. All of our differences and all of our disagreements went away during that ride to the jail.

When we arrived at the jail, we sat silently in the parking lot for a while. I was scared, and my dad could tell. I remember him saying, "Son, we will get this all figured out. Just be strong." It was time to face the music and the consequences of my actions. I gave him a big hug right before the steel door of the jail cell slammed shut. I had no idea at that moment, but it would be a long time before I would hug my dad again as a free man. Through the window of the door, I could see the pain in his eyes, and I could sense the unconditional love that he had for me. However, the unconditional love from my father would have no impact or authority over the new world I had just entered.

I sat in the county jail for almost three months waiting to see if the teen I had injured would come out of his coma or not. They revoked my bond as the authorities waited to see if the teen would live or die. They wanted to see if the attempted murder charge would stick or if they needed to charge me with something far worse. I celebrated my eighteenth birthday in jail as I awaited the outcome. I missed a lot during this time. It was my senior year in high school, and prom had been right around the corner. I struggled knowing all that I was missing on the outside. I wanted to go back so desperately and change things, not just what had happened the night on the beach, but every moment leading up to it. What made my stay in county jail even harder was the fear of the unknown.

I waited it out in what had to be the worst county jail in all of the United States. Morgan Street County Jail at the time was a gladiator school, meaning every day was a fight for survival. Most county jails have a guard station centered in the pod with twenty-four-hour surveillance. Not at this jail. The way it was set up, the guards had no idea what was happening in the cells. They only came by every few hours to count or to serve meals. This left a lot of time unsupervised and a lot of time for bad things to happen. And believe me, they did. I called home every week, pleading with my parents to get me out of the hell I was in, but unfortunately their hands were tied.

As I write this now, I can't help imagining the helplessness my parents must have felt. If you recall, just a few years prior, they had experienced a similar helpless feeling surrounding my sister's situation. This test would prove to be much greater for them because of the duration of time that was before them. I believe God uses situations in our lives, the good and the bad, to help us grow. He uses times in our lives to strengthen us for the times ahead. I believe what my parents had gone through a few years earlier with Stephanie prepared them for what they were going through at that time with me and what they were later going to go through as the situation played out.

My parents dipped into their savings to hire an attorney for me. He turned out to be a horrible attorney, to say the least. He rarely visited me in jail, and I felt he wasn't doing the activities an attorney was supposed to do. After I had spent two months in jail, he had not even taken a statement from me yet and had failed to contact my friends like Marks who had been with me that evening on the beach. But despite the lack of proper representation, after roughly three months behind bars, I heard the news I had so desperately wanted to hear.

My victim had come out of his coma. This was the best news I had heard in a long time. An ounce of hope sparked within me; maybe we both would be able to get on with our lives soon. Unfortunately, the price had not yet been paid for the decision I had made that Friday night three months before. For me, this journey was just beginning. For three more months, attorneys would do their depositions and their discoveries, file their motions, and so on. All the while, I battled to survive the hell called Morgan Street County Jail.

After almost six months, the case came to a head. Despite the hundreds of letters written on my behalf, the decision was made that would seal my fate. For the fateful night on the beach and the choice I had made, I would be sentenced to ten years in Florida State Prison. On the day of sentencing, the courtroom was filled with my friends and family. They had tears in their eyes and were in shock and disbelief as they watched me take my fall—the fall of a life that had had such a bright future ahead, filled with opportunity. Now my life had a future filled with uncertainty and fear. The journey into an uncertain future was just beginning for many of the people in that courtroom as well.

For me the day in the courtroom was the day my dreams were sentenced to death. As I hugged my family one last time before the authorities carried me away, I felt an overwhelming feeling that all I had hoped for and dreamed for in my life was gone. Prior to that fateful Friday night on the beach, I was still on track to fulfill those dreams, even though I had made some poor decisions and had become unfocused, even though the influences in my life at the time were not influencing me in the right direction. And even though my passion and discipline had wavered, my dream of playing football one day was still there and still alive. Before the events of that night, everything I hoped for was still possible. But things had changed since that Friday night.

As I walked out of the courtroom, I dropped my head, for I knew my dream was no longer a possibility. As a matter of fact, my dream to play football was the last thing on my mind. All I wanted at that moment was to have my freedom; nothing else mattered. Shock being the feeling I recall the most, it was as if I was stuck in a bad dream. I felt that at any moment I would wake up and still have my whole life ahead of me. It's hard to describe the emptiness I felt as I was escorted through the corridor and back to the holding cell. As I sat there in the holding cell, I began to cry. I cried for my family. Even though I knew they were leaving that courtroom to go back to their lives, what lives were they going back to? I knew my parents had been sentenced in that courtroom as well. And I knew their lives would never be the same.

Chapter 4

Behind the Fence

BEHIND THE FENCE

A FEW WEEKS later, I was awakened at around three o'clock in the morning and told by the guard to pack my stuff. I was leaving, and all of the thoughts about prison that had prevented me from sleeping at night were about to become reality. As I loaded the only belongings I had into a pillowcase, I tried to ready myself for the unknown and for the very scary journey that lay ahead. Outside of the cell in the hallway, I noticed a line of inmates with pillowcases in hand. They obviously held the same fate as my own, and I took my place in the line of murderers, rapists, and thugs. We were escorted to a large garage, where we were shackled from head to toe. I will never forget the feeling of that cold steel being attached to my ankles and wrists. A long chain connected the shackles from our wrists to our ankles, and the setup prevented us from even scratching our nose and made it painful to walk. We were then loaded onto a large gray bus with steel mesh over the windows.

It was so quiet on the bus you could hear a pin drop. Maybe everyone was still asleep, being that it was 3:00 a.m. But I couldn't help thinking the quietness was the calm before the storm. I'm sure most were like me—too nervous to speak. Or maybe they, like me, were anticipating what waited on the other end of that bus ride. The large steel garage door of the jail lifted, and we headed off into the darkness. I had no idea where we were headed, but I knew it was a place far from home and far from all that I held dear.

After a three- or four-hour journey, just as the sun peaked over the trees, we arrived at our destination. The prison was tucked deep in the woods of North Florida, hours from my home. The first thing I noticed were the rows upon rows of razor wire blanketing a twenty-foot-high fence that surrounded the compound. About ten feet inside the fence was another fence; it, too, was blanketed with razor wire from top to bottom. The two fences were so thick with this wire that we still could not see inside the compound. The interior was still a mystery from this view, and the fences were a painful reminder that once we were on the inside, we were there to stay.

As we unloaded the bus and headed toward the gate, the fence was lined with inmates yelling out various expletives welcoming us to our new home. I heard one yell out, "Hey, cracker, I'll see you on the inside." I looked around and noticed that I was one of few "crackers" in the line. I assumed he had directed it toward me, and I began to prepare myself mentally for what was to come. I came prepared to fight; if I ever returned home, it was going to be with my dignity intact. I was prepared to do that at all costs, even if it meant putting my life on the line. I had made a choice to fight one Friday night, and because of that choice, I was going to fight without any choice at all.

We were ushered into a large room, where we were lined up in a long straight line shoulder to shoulder. Our numbers reached into the hundred marks. We were then instructed to strip from head to toe so we could be searched for contraband. There was a certain humility felt when we were lined up there in the nude and were told to stick out our tongues, run our fingers through our hair, and bend over and spread 'em.

"When pride comes, then comes disgrace, but with the humble is wisdom" (Prov. 11:2).

I could already tell from the tonality of the guards that my fellow inmates were not all I would have to fear in this place. The guards were loud, belligerent, and disrespectful. Even my toughest football coach never spoke to me the way those guards did. The guards wanted to make a statement right off the bat that they were in charge.

I came to realize the harshness of my environment on that very first day. It was count time, and I was part of what is called an open-bay dorm. It is a large building with rows and rows of bunks on top of one another. I imagined it was much like military barracks at a boot camp. Hundreds of inmates could be housed in one of these dormitories. These count times were brutal. Each inmate would have to sit on his bunk erect with his hands on his knees and facing forward. These count times lasted as long as two hours at times. Talking was not permitted, and if you even slouched your shoulders during this time, you would be reprimanded.

I wasn't sure at the time what "reprimanded" meant, but I was not willing to find out. I sat facing forward, with my hands on my knees, scared to even look around. I soon found out how serious a consequence one might pay if he did not follow the protocol of count time.

About ten bunks ahead of me on a top bunk was a young black kid who had decided he was going to buck the system.

About an hour into the count time, he decided he would lie down. I remember hearing one of the inmates on the bunk next to him say, "Man, you better sit up." He ignored the warning. A few moments later, a guard entered the dorm to address the insubordinate kid. After a brief exchange of words, it became obvious the kid was not going to budge.

The guard radioed for backup, and within a few minutes, several guards came rushing through the door of the dorm prepared for battle. When they came like that, they came with force. The young man was given a final warning, and when he refused, one of the guards standing behind him grabbed him from behind by the collar of his shirt and snatched him from the bunk. He fell from the top bunk and landed directly on his head.

From ten rows back, I could hear his neck snap as he hit the floor. It was obvious the guards had heard it as well, as they stood in silence for a moment looking at his lifeless body lying on the floor. After a moment they grabbed him by the feet and dragged him out of the dorm. I'm not sure what happened afterward, but we never saw or heard from that kid again.

This prison was called a reception center; it was the first stop of many on this prison journey. This was the place that they had designed to and hoped would break your spirits, making you a more manageable inmate during the rest of your sentence. There would be no contact from here with the outside world. There was no mail, no phones, and no visitation.

For three months in hell, I did not speak to or hear from my family. My mom and dad experienced the fear of not knowing where I was, what I was going through, or even if I were still alive. I thought about my mom every day and the anxiety she must have been experiencing. I felt extreme guilt inside for a decision I had made that caused her and my father so much worry and so much pain.

I became like a robot at that place. I kept to myself and watched everything going on around me. I knew I only had about three months to survive here, and because of that, I went into survival mode.

One day I noticed a hill on the backside of the prison just outside the fence. On this hill rested a blanket of tombstones. In this graveyard belonged bodies of inmates who had died or had been killed inside the fence. These were the bodies that had never been claimed by any family for proper burial. The prison made sure the cemetery was in plain view for all to see. It became a simple reminder that this place could be the end if we weren't careful. It was a reminder that life is precious and so are the choices that we make. I had three months to keep myself from becoming part of that hill.

I say three months because we were informed when we arrived that this would only be our temporary home. This was the place where we would become oriented to prison life before being transferred to our permanent institution. We were told the orientation process would take three months to complete. The prison called it an orientation process, but I referred to it as the breakdown process. This three-month orientation was designed to break our spirits. And for the weak at heart, the prison system would accomplish its goal.

After three months I was transferred to a prison only forty-five minutes from my home. This move brought with it the first contact I had with my family in over three months. I called my parents upon arriving, and as soon as we heard one another's voices, the tears began to flow. I buried my face in the wall as my tears flowed; I could not show any weakness in my new place.

Both my parents and I were extremely happy that we had made contact and that I had been transferred so close to home. The distance would allow my family to visit more conveniently on the weekends. We both needed to have that close contact for so many reasons. Our very short and very emotional phone call ended, and then it was back to business. You see, the luxury of being close to home came with a price. I had been transferred to another gladiator school. It was one of the worst prisons in Florida, and surviving there would be a test greater than anything I had yet faced.

Because of my age, I had been transferred to a youthful offender prison. The age group ranged from sixteen- to twenty-one-year-olds. Because of the ages of the inmates in this facility, there was a lack of maturity in this type of environment. My fellow inmates had a lack of respect for authority, a lack of respect for one another, and a lack of respect for human life in general. If you combine all of these factors into one environment that is only somewhat controlled, it becomes a recipe for disaster. In this place, you didn't have to go out looking for trouble; the trouble came looking for you.

The institution had its own economy, and it had its own rules. The rules and this economy were ruled and riddled by gang violence. Just stepping out of my cell every day posed the opportunity to get caught up in something I did not want to get caught up in. There was a lot of violence at this prison, and riots were a regular occurrence there. I never knew when violence would happen or whether I would be in the wrong place when it did. The things I witnessed hurt my heart to the core, and fear governed my every step. Like most in this situation, the opportunity to fight for my life and my survival came on many occasions. Once I had proven that I was a gladiator also, word spread, and the altercations came further and further apart.

However, there was never a day I didn't walk with eyes in the back of my head, always prepared and always ready. It was a life I did not want to live, but it was the life I had created by the choices I had made. There was no one to blame but myself. I longed for an escape from this hell, and I longed to have my life back. But I had really just begun my journey. I had so much time ahead of me at that point.

The daily routine there was much like the day before, so much so that I really couldn't tell one day from the last. Most of the time, I did not even know what day of the week it was. The last thing I wanted to look at was a calendar. With a ten-year sentence, looking at a calendar would only remind me of how much time I still had to do. Every day here started the same and ended the same. And this particular day had ended like all of the rest. As I resigned to my cell for the night, I did not know that this night would be different from any other.

Chapter 5

The Light in the Darkness

The Light in the Darkness

It was dark and cold in the cell. The only light I saw was the light from the catwalk shining in beneath the large cell door. I crouched down in the corner of the room and pulled my knees tightly to my chest. As I heard the yells and screams around me, I almost felt a sense of security in that cell. This was the night that changed everything in my life. This was the night I described earlier, when the weight of the world came crashing in on me. This was the night when the flood of emotions completely overtook me and brought me to a new understanding.

When I saw the light shining under the door, I became convicted. The light was standing out in the darkness. The darkness had no power over the light coming in beneath the door. I began to think back to things I had heard on Sundays when my mother would drag us all to church. I recalled statements like "the enemy of darkness is light!"

> "The light shines in the darkness, and the darkness has not overcome it" (John 1:5).

I had heard these types of things said before—the contrast between the darkness and the light. But come on, light versus dark and dark versus light? Good versus evil? Let's face it; a light penetrating beneath the door was not going to free me. I began to chuckle a little bit as I realized what was happening to me. Yep, I was sure of it...I was losing my mind. *Great,* I thought. *I'm going to get shipped off to one of those psychiatric prisons where they pump you full of Thorazine every day.* Soon I would be walking around all day doing the "Thorazine Shuffle" and staring off into space.

Luckily that wouldn't be the case for me, because I wasn't losing my mind at all. As a matter of fact, things began to get very clear.

"'to give light to those who sit in darkness and in the shadow of death, to guide our feet into the way of peace'" (Luke 1:79).

I was being given a message in the darkness. In the midst of all of the thoughts going through my head, I remembered something my grandfather had said to me when I was a little boy. As a child, I spent most of my summers at my grandparents' farm in a little town just south of Tallahassee, Florida. They had hundreds of acres of plush woods, fresh ponds to swim in, and a lot of animals. It was an awesome place for any kid to spend his summers. During those summers my grandfather and I would hunt, fish, and work on the farm. We shared quality time together that I will never forget.

My grandfather was a godly man, and every morning at breakfast he would read devotions to us while we ate. He was always preaching to me during those summer visits. I would just agree with him by saying, "OK, Granddaddy," but most of it would go in one ear and out the other. As a child, I was only concerned with having fun—I had my own agenda. I was in no way, shape, or form interested in all of the "religious talk," but little did I know, my granddaddy had planted a seed those many years ago.

One of those summers, he said to me, "Son, promise me one thing. When you're at your darkest moment in life, your back's against the wall, and you don't feel like you have any way out, drop to your knees immediately and cry out for Jesus." I just replied, "OK, Granddaddy." I had blown him off as usual—or had I? I never thought about that conversation again until that night in the prison cell.

I was there, and I was sure of it. I was in the darkest time of my life, my back was against the wall, and I didn't feel like I had any way out. What did I have to lose? So I took Granddaddy's advice, and I spun around onto my knees and laid my cheek on the cold, dirty, concrete prison floor. If I could have gotten lower, I would have. Being on that floor symbolized the level I had reached in my life. The concrete floor was hard to my face and knees, causing immediate discomfort. I was at rock bottom. I was hopeless, helpless, scared, and lonely. There I knelt alone, with my face buried against a dirty prison floor and probably losing my mind. And in that moment, I did what my granddaddy made me promise him so many years ago. I cried out for God.

I cried like I had never cried before. I cried out to God, and I said, "God, I believe that you are real, and, God, I can't do this without you. Please take over my life, and please take over my heart. Please open my eyes, please open my ears, and please give me understanding and wisdom. Help me to understand my purpose and to understand what I am supposed to do with my life. Please protect me and help me to get out of this place alive. Give me peace during this time that I am here. Help me to develop a relationship with you so that I can understand how you want me to live my life. All I thought I wanted in my life is nonexistent, and I feel lost. Please take over my life and guide my path. In Jesus's name I pray."

I remained there on the floor, almost paralyzed, for a few moments. Still with my eyes closed, I sensed a bright light around me, almost like someone had opened the door of the cellblock, allowing all of the light from the corridor to rush in. But no one was around. I felt warmth come over my body as if I were lying next to a campfire, and I felt a sense of peace overtake me. Instantly in that moment, I was no longer scared, and I no longer feared for my life. Somehow, someway, I knew I would be protected from that moment on. I was no longer depressed, and I felt a strength inside of me that gave me an amazing sense of hope. As I thought of all the time I still had to do, I felt peace knowing God was preparing me for something, and I could feel His presence inside of me.

Immediately the communication started. He said to me that I was going to be there for a while, but that when I was done, I was going to do great things. I knew immediately that the plans I had for my life were not the plans that He had, and I had peace in knowing that. I had peace knowing that He was now in control and I need not worry anymore. I felt a feeling of openness and excitement. All of a sudden, I felt excited for my life again. I knew something great was going to happen in my life. I realized that my life was not over and that the place I was in was only temporary. I understood that night on the floor that I was there in prison for a reason. I understood that God was going to use my situation in some way for His glory, and I felt excited knowing that He would reveal that to me in due time.

The floor was no longer cold to my face, and my knees no longer hurt from the hardness of the concrete. I had not lost my mind. Instead, I had just experienced a moment I had only heard of but never quite believed. That night everything changed. God also revealed to me that there had been a battle going on for my life. There was good and evil, and there were two forces pursuing my life and my heart. And the battle for my life was just heating up.

I was still in a dark place, surrounded by the enemy. I was surrounded by an enemy that I was sure would never give up. And now I had a new understanding of it all. Even though I had a new lease on life and I knew God was with me, I still needed to do my part. After all, I was still in prison. I needed to survive that place if I was ever going to find my purpose. I wanted to make sure I didn't do anything stupid to get myself killed while I was there.

To survive, I began to study people. I wanted to truly understand what made people tick—what made people do the things they did and make the decisions they made. I wanted to know who I should mess with and who I should not mess with. I thought if I could figure out how to get along with everyone, then I would have nothing to worry about. I watched everything that went on around me. I watched people interact with one another every day, and I could quickly pinpoint the people who lacked integrity and those who did not. In watching the different personalities around me, I learned how to interact with them as well. And soon an opportunity was given to me that took my understanding of people to a whole new level.

One day I was called to Mr. Pass's office. Mr. Pass was a classification officer at the prison. Classification officers were civilians who worked for the state. They were assigned inmates to oversee and guide during the inmates' stay. Their responsibilities included creating a plan of action for development and direction for the inmates. Classification officers were also in charge of disciplinary action for those inmates who violated the rules. So when I was called to Mr. Pass's office, I immediately thought the worst. I began to question what I had done wrong. But little did I know, God was already flexing His muscles and making moves on my behalf.

I was nervous as Mr. Pass peered across the desk at me with my file in his hand. He said, "Steve, I have viewed your file, and there is something different about you. I don't believe you are supposed to be in this place, and I want to help you. I want to create a plan for you that is going to involve a lot of self-development. My goal is to help you so that when you leave this place, you will never come back. I have a feeling that when you leave here, you will go and do great things." I knew the moment he said it that God was confirming what He had said to me in the cell that night.

Mr. Pass's plan of action was to enroll me into a very strict twelve-month self-development program called Tier. Because this program was so strict and regimented, only the most well-behaved inmates were allowed to participate. God was putting me in the program for a reason. But at the time, I had no idea why.

The Tier program had its own separate dormitory on the compound. All inmates participating in the program were housed in this dorm, separate from the rest of the general population. That meant I would be moving, and it also meant I would be getting a cellmate.

At first glance my new cellmate, Bill, was a short little puny guy. My first thought was that he had joined the program to get away from the dangers of the compound. Because the program was separate from the rest of the population, some guys would join just to be in a safer environment. I felt this had to be the case for Bill. Man, was I wrong. Bill was a stick of dynamite, and he received a high level of respect from the other inmates. They respected him for many reasons, and after being in the dorm with him for a short time, I realized why.

Bill was what they called a peer counselor. He had been in the program for a while and had proven he was not your normal inmate. Bill had absorbed all the Tier program was teaching and had truly become a leader in the group. He was the voice of reason, and he rallied the troops, inspiring true change in their lives. And with my newfound desire to change, he quickly became someone I looked up to.

Over the next several months, Bill and I became the best of friends. He shared with me insight that was outside the teaching of normal prison life. He shared with me his outlook on life, his desire to make a difference, and his desire to live a different way. It was no surprise to me to find out that Bill, too, was a believer. When a man is right in his heart with God, you can usually tell. And with Bill, this was definitely the case. He wasn't one to preach, but his actions let you know.

Bill had been the ringleader of a pretty dangerous gang on the streets. He was not the guy you would want to cross. And his reputation on the streets had followed him behind the fence, creating a high level of respect for him from the other inmates. Little did they know, Bill was no longer that man. It never fails to amaze me how drastically God can change a man's heart.

"'And I will give them one heart, and put a new spirit within them. I will remove the heart of stone from their flesh...'" (Ezek. 11:19).

God had taken Bill's leadership from the streets and had redirected it for good. Bill was my best friend and my mentor. He would soon be released. I will never forget the day he left. It was a bittersweet event, as I was happy to see him going home, but also sad to know that I would no longer have my friend with me. After all, we had become like brothers. Bill went on to do exactly what he said he was going to do. He has lived a successful life since his release. He got married and has three beautiful children. As a matter of fact, his wife is my first cousin, whom I introduced to him while we were still behind the fence. And yes, he is still to this day my best friend and brother, still mentoring me and encouraging me every step of the way.

Bill's mentorship behind the fence paid off for me. I engaged wholeheartedly into the program, and after I completed the program, they asked me to be a peer counselor. I was given the chance to mentor to and inspire other inmates to a life of change. I picked up right where Bill had left off. Through that experience I came to develop a passion for self-development that would manifest and grow for the rest of my life. Every step of the way, I could see God working in my life. So many times throughout my incarceration, God showed Himself to me, not only through the experiences but also through the people He put in my life. With every experience and around every corner I turned there, I knew that He was with me. I believed that I had entered into an irrevocable contract with God, and I knew in my heart He would never leave me.

I learned a lot from the program and being a mentor to others. For the next several years, I ate, drank, and slept self-development material. It was a rewarding time as I watched my influence change the course and direction of many men's lives in there. Something within me was starting to manifest. I was being prepared for something, and at the time I did not know what that something was.

> "'For I know the plans I have for you,' declares the Lord, 'plans to prosper you and not to harm you, plans to give you hope and a future'" (Jer. 29:11).

Doing the time was hard, as I missed so many things that were taking place on the outside. I missed my high school prom and graduation. I missed college and all of the experiences that could have come from it. I missed family events, such as holidays, weddings, and children being born. My sister got married and gave birth to my niece all while I was behind the fence. My mom and dad went through many changes over the years as well. But they never missed a holiday with me. Their world and their plans always revolved around being there for me. I will never forget the time my mom tried to bring me a cake for my birthday. Apparently she had never seen any of those prison movies where someone sneaks a file into a cake. But the guards had...and they didn't find it very funny. She meant well, and she didn't know any better, and luckily, they did not throw me in the hole for that.

On that cold and dirty prison floor years before, I had asked God to deliver me from prison and to restore my life. And after having served almost seven years of my ten-year sentence, God answered that prayer. It had been a long and hard seven years of my life. I had been there from the age of seventeen to the age of twenty-four. I had learned so many valuable lessons along the way. I had fought for my sanity, I had fought not to become institutionalized, and I had fought for my life. I had survived, and I was about to start my life again.

My family stayed supportive and loyal to me throughout the entire seven years. They were an absolute blessing to me during the toughest of times. And in April 2001, they were waiting for me outside those gates with open arms and eyes filled with tears of joy. Even my cousin and my best pal Bill were there to welcome me home. It's hard to describe the feeling I felt as I walked out of that prison. I wanted to drop to my knees and kiss the ground. I was free at last!

Recently I was speaking with my mom about the time during my incarceration. She recalled the heartbreak she experienced every time she had to leave after visiting me. She described standing in the parking lot at the prison watching me through the fence as I disappeared back into the compound. Her joy on the day of my release was overwhelming; I could feel it from her embrace. On that day the people who had supported me became free as well.

I was excited and also nervous about my new freedom; my life was truly about to start over. I held tightly to the fact that God had guided me throughout the entire experience and that He would continue to guide me as I moved forward with my life. It was going to be a life with no more fences, no more cold and dark prison cells, and no more regret.

Faith is why I'm here today and faith
is why I made it through.
—JONATHAN ANTHONY BURKETT

Chapter 6

The Second Fall

THE SECOND FALL

GETTING BACK TO life was not going to be an easy task, because so much had changed. I left as a seventeen-year-old kid, and now I was a twenty-four-year-old man. But immediately God started to open doors in my life. I quickly found out that there are not a lot of job opportunities available for ex-convicts. You can either go into construction or sell used cars. I had done enough hard labor in the hot Florida sun while behind the fence; I was ready to soak up some air-conditioning.

During the last several months of my incarceration, I had a pen pal. My aunt owned a small day-care center in the town I was from. Being the loving and supportive aunt that she was, she had a picture of me on her desk. One of the girls working there inquired about my photo one day. After she heard my story and showed interest, my aunt suggested she write me a letter. After months of correspondence, our friendship had progressed into stronger feelings. She even got on my visitation list and visited me frequently. When I was released from prison, she and I began to court.

Her brother was the general manager for a large used car outfit. He claimed he could get past the background check and give me the chance I needed. I began working for the company and quickly progressed through the corporate ranks. Within a couple of years, I was flown to the corporate office in Phoenix, Arizona, where I was offered a position as a corporate sales trainer. I accredit my success to all of the self-development and coaching I received while incarcerated. This new position gave me the chance to travel all over the country and to experience many new things.

Things in my life couldn't be better. I traveled to dealerships that were struggling and got them back on the right track. I was making great money, but more importantly, I was doing what I loved, and that was motivating people. I purchased my very first home on a nice piece of land, and the relationship with the girl who had supported me during the last several months of my incarceration had progressed into something more serious.

It felt like everything in my life was moving in the right direction. I began to feel like I finally had my life in order and that I was back in control of my own destiny. There was just one big problem with that: I thought I was in control. As I developed my relationship with God behind the fence, it had strengthened my faith that He was in complete control of my life. But somehow with everything going well in my life and feeling like I was in control of it all, my relationship with God started to suffer. What I had experienced in prison had almost at this point become a distant memory, and along with it, unfortunately, the relationship that I had with God. I wasn't attending church, I wasn't reading my Bible, and I wasn't praying. I was doing things in my life my way, and it wasn't long before things started to fall apart at the seams.

My relationship with the girl who had stood by me during my incarceration came to an end. I soon began to engage in after-hours partying with the guys from work, and man, those car guys knew how to party. Even though I was still doing well financially and seemed to be having a great time in the process, I was lost. For some reason I had plenty of friends, but I was still alone. And then one night I met a young lady who seemed to be on the same path of fun and excitement that I was.

We immediately hit it off and spent almost every spare second together. Within a short period of time, she stole my heart, and I was head over heels in love. They say love is blind, and I gave a whole new meaning to that statement. I became blinded to everything else in my life. I was blind to my family, my job, and my responsibilities. Even more importantly, I was blind to the relationship that I had once had with God. I was focused solely and completely on being with this girl and making her happy.

My life became an absolutely hot mess. I was behind the wheel of my life, and I had it all under control...or so I thought. In reality I was on a reckless path, without God in my life. My relationship with this girl was reckless and volatile from very early on. Three months into the relationship, we had a blowout fight that would mark its end. However, the repercussions of my irresponsibility and reckless behavior would be revealed to me soon enough.

A few weeks after the breakup, I received a phone call from her one day informing me that she needed to talk. I had no idea at that moment what she wanted to talk about, but I agreed to go over. As I sat on the couch, I could tell by her seriousness that she was searching for the words to tell me what was on her mind. After what seemed to be an eternity of silence, she informed me that she was pregnant.

A flood of emotions immediately overcame me. In that moment, I felt excitement, fear, doubt, and complete uncertainty. I was in shock, to say the least. But weren't we on a break? Our relationship had ended. In just a short period of time, we had already proved that we were not compatible with each other.

So immediately the question arose: should we bring this child into this world or not? Immediately a voice inside of me spoke up. It was a voice I hadn't heard in quite a while. Upon hearing this voice, I knew the only right choice was to keep the baby. But what were we going to do about our relationship? After much discussion and what seemed to be an unexpected turn of events, we decided we should give our relationship another try.

I was raised as a good ol' Southern boy, so a month after hearing the news of the pregnancy, I proposed to her, and within two months, we were married. Five months later, she gave birth to a beautiful little girl. Even with an amazing gift from God in our lives, not a whole lot changed in our relationship. Our marriage was still volatile and unhealthy, bringing out the worst in both of us. For quite a while, that little girl was the thread that held it all together. But what were we holding onto? The fact of the matter is that I didn't have God in my life, and we didn't have God in our marriage. This made it very difficult to make things work.

But yet we continued to hold on. The stress of an unhappy marriage started to affect my job and ultimately started to affect our finances as well. And because we were still living our lives irresponsibly and out of control, she got pregnant again. Two years into the relationship, we had another little girl on the way.

During her pregnancy, we separated and got back together on a few occasions. We just never could seem to get it right.

Then, just as things seemed like they couldn't get any worse, they did. I was called into the office one day by my regional manager. He delivered me some news that turned my world upside down. "With much regret," he said, "we have to let you go." It was 2006, and things in the economy were already changing for the worse. The company had closed numerous dealerships and was making cuts. Unfortunately for me, one of the first cuts is usually the trainers.

I begged and pleaded, and even shed a few tears. I had been with the company for over five years; I had worked countless hours and spent time away from my family. I had a baby on the way and no money saved—how could they do this to me? It was a devastating experience, to say the least. I recall driving around town aimlessly for hours afterward. I drove down streets I had never been down before, without a destination in mind. I did not want to go home; I did not want to tell my wife that I had lost my job. We were already having so many problems, and I just knew this news would be the icing on the cake. Our financial situation quickly went from bad to worse.

Reality hit...I was an ex-convict with no college education. Finding a job that would replace the high level of income I had at the time was nearly impossible. Very quickly I started to lose all of the material things in my life: my house and land, my fancy truck, and all the various toys I had accumulated during my success. And ultimately—we already knew this was coming—my marriage came to an end. I believe the financial stress on top of an already struggling marriage became the straw that broke the camel's back. Without God's presence in our marriage, we were unable to overcome our differences.

This final separation was just the beginning of a long and hard road ahead. She and I could not get along when we were together, and starting a divorce with two children involved created a whole new level of dispute. She wanted to have full custody of the girls, and I refused to be an every-other-weekend dad. So the battle began. When I received a summons for the very first court appearance, I recalled the last time I had stepped into a courtroom. The verdict that day was a verdict that had changed my life forever and had turned my world upside down. I did not want my life to fall mercy to the court system once again.

So I went out and hired a very successful divorce attorney in town to represent me. Now I was truly stuck between a rock and a hard place. I had lost my job, I had lost my home, and I had lost just about everything I had. I was broke, and attorneys are expensive. *How will I ever be able to afford this?* I wondered. Luckily for me, I had amazing friends and family who offered me financial assistance during those tough times. Had it not been for their support, I'm not sure how things might have turned out.

However, having attorneys involved in your personal matters is not always the best decision, either. Things between my wife and I got much worse before they got any better. Our divorce became an ugly and bitter battle. At times I felt like the battle was never going to end. How had it come to this? How had I gotten to the place I was at in my life? The thought of losing my children in the midst of everything else I had lost became unbearable. What I was going through at that time was harder emotionally than the years I spent behind bars.

Life is at its best when everything has fallen out of place, and you decide that you're going to fight to get them right, not when everything is going your way and everyone is praising you.
—Thisuri Wanniarachchi

Like in prison, this time in my life once again brought me to my knees. One night I sat at my house in the dark, alone and depressed. I crouched down in the corner of the room and pulled my knees to my chest. I dropped my face in shame and cried. Sound familiar?

Yes, I had been there before. And just like the time before, I was scared for the future. There I was again, in the darkness, my back against the wall, and I didn't feel like I had any way out. I thought about all of the mistakes I had made and the people I had hurt. I thought about all of the bad choices leading up to that moment. But this time was different, because it wasn't just about me. There were two little girls involved whom I loved more than anything in this world.

As I sat there in tears, I thought about how my choices and actions were going to affect their lives. Being unable to make it work for their sake was breaking my heart. Once again in the dark, during one of the darkest moments of my life, I recalled my grandfather's advice from so many years before. I spun around onto my knees and laid my face on the floor. I cried like I had never cried before.

This time as I laid my face on the floor and cried, I didn't plead with God to take over my life. Instead, I pleaded with Him to take me back. For seven years in hell, He held my hand. He gave me peace, He gave me understanding, and He gave me purpose. And as soon as all those blessings started to manifest themselves in my life, I forgot. I pulled away from Him, and I stopped showing Him the love and the gratitude and the glory that He deserved.

How could I have had my eyes so open at one point and then become so blind? I had been blinded by love or lust or whatever it was. I had been blinded by success, money, and material things. I felt humiliated as I lay there on the floor, and I begged for forgiveness with all of my heart. *Why would He forgive me?* I wondered. *How many chances did I deserve? What a fool I had been.*

> Seek the Lord while He may be found, call upon him while He is near. Let the wicked forsake his way, and the unrighteous man his thoughts; let him return to the Lord, and He will have mercy on him; and to our God, for He will abundantly pardon (Isa. 55:6–7).

Again in my darkest hour, God's love overtook me. Like in the prison cell that night, I instantly felt peace. I wasn't scared anymore for what the future held, because I knew that God was still there. As a matter of fact, in that moment I knew that He had never left me. Once again my eyes were opened, and I could see the error of my ways. I knew God had allowed me to make my own choices and to make my own bed hard. But He was right there to lift me back up when I called out His name.

Just like before I knew I needed to do my part, and I knew I had a long road ahead. In order to do my part, I needed to make some major changes in my life. I needed to pick myself up and get refocused. Not only had I turned my focus away from God, but I had stopped the self-development I had become so passionate about during my time away. I began to read and reengage in bettering myself from the inside out. Once I realized my mistakes and gave myself a checkup from the neck up, things started to change. With new focus and a new understanding, positive things started to happen pretty quickly.

One of the most positive things that happened to me around this time was a beautiful young lady named Lauren. I'd known Lauren for a few years through mutual friends and had always known that there was something different and special about her. She was one of those people whom you just knew you could count on. She was beautiful, smart, responsible, and giving. She had always been and continued to be a very positive influence in my life. Lauren had been married previously and was going through her own separation and divorce at the same time that I was.

She and I began to spend more time together, and we leaned on each other during the tough times we were both experiencing. Our friendship and support for each other continued to grow and strengthen. She was someone I loved talking to and spending time with. My two little girls took a special liking to her as well, and my younger daughter even nicknamed her "Winnie." Obviously at the time, I was going through a very difficult time with my bitter divorce and child custody battle. I knew without a shadow of a doubt that Lauren being in my life was not by chance.

As time moved on, our relationship grew into something much more powerful. I looked at her and realized that the type of relationship she and I had was the way a relationship was supposed to be. One night at the house, a song called "Broken Road" by Rascal Flatts came on the radio. I asked her to dance, and the rest is history. I fell deeply in love with her, and in doing so, I realized what true love really felt like.

Lauren was a Christian as well and had a desire to deepen her own relationship with God. It was obvious to me very quickly that God was once again flexing His muscles and showing off.

> Whatever you ask in my name, this I will do, that the Father may be glorified in the Son. If you ask anything in my name, I will do it (John 14:13–14).

All too often we lean unto our own understanding of things. Events and situations in our lives take place, and we question why they happened the way they did. I've found that when we ask for things in our lives, God always gives us more than we asked for—something better than what we have envisioned. For me Lauren was better than anything I had asked Him for. God once again proved to me that He is always in control and has a plan for everything.

Lauren and I had to work through some tough situations in the beginning of our relationship with my divorce and custody battle still going on. But with the newfound strength and rekindling of my relationship with God, my heart started to change toward my ex-wife. The bitterness that I felt toward her began to subside. I believe that God started to change her heart as well. One day after what had been a long, hard, and expensive battle, we decided to stop the fight. We agreed to share custody of the girls and to move forward with raising them to the best of our abilities.

God had carried me through another storm.

Chapter 7

Something Missing

Something Missing

With both of our divorces behind us, Lauren and I were relieved and excited to continue our journey together. Our relationship continued to strengthen, and our love deepened with each new day. We continued to stay focused on deepening our individual relationships with God and keeping Him at the center of our relationship. In doing so, many more blessings came our way. Lauren and I moved in together and were fully engaged in our relationship, and then the unexpected happened. Lauren had failed to have any children during her first marriage. The doctors had told her that she would not be able to have kids, but God had a different plan. In 2008 Lauren gave birth to a beautiful little girl that we named Katie. Now we had three little girls—Chloe, Cory, and Katie. I was in a house full of females, and life was full of excitement and new experiences.

My dad gave me a hard time about having another girl. He would make perverted jokes about what it took to make a boy and how I must be falling short in that department. Even though his granddaughters melted his heart and he loved them very much, I knew he wanted a grandson.

Over the next year, my dad became very sick. A few years prior, he had been diagnosed with diabetes. Unwilling to conform to a strict diet, he became progressively worse, and my mother and sister became his full-time caregivers. My relationship with my dad had been a healthy one since my release from prison. We spent a lot of time together, and I talked with him almost every day. Before he became sick, he and I would play golf together frequently. I valued my time on the course with him. After all, we had a lot of lost time to make up for. I was thankful for the relationship that my father and I had developed. He had become one of my best pals, and I always looked to him for advice. Our disputes from the past did not matter to us anymore. He found joy in my successes, and I was happy to make him proud. We loved each other dearly.

In April 2010, my dad took his last breath at the age of sixty years old. He went in for a pretty simple surgery that most people would survive. However, because of the diabetes, he received an infection that hit his bloodstream and ended his life. It was one of the most painful moments of my life. I remember sitting at his bedside, asking him if he knew the Lord. Thankfully he said he did, and we prayed together. My dad had never been a person to openly speak about his faith; therefore, I had to ask him the question. I could not imagine losing my father knowing that he had never made that decision. I needed to have that peace of mind before I let him go. Losing my father was the second time in life that I truly began to think about purpose. I wondered what my father's purpose was. I wondered if he knew what it was and if he had fulfilled it, or if he had taken it to the grave with him.

Like his faith, I never heard him speak about purpose. The loss of my father caused me to question my own purpose in life again. What was I supposed to do with my talents, time, and treasures? "What had God been preparing me for?" I asked, but the answer did not come. I look back now and truly believe that the answer did not come because I was not ready at the time. God reveals to us our purpose when He's ready to. God has to develop the dreamer before He can develop the dream. I believe God will reveal our purpose to us when He knows that we can handle it. He will not halfway prepare us for something as important as the reason He created us. There was still more to learn.

Our vision is so limited we can hardly imagine a love that does not show itself in protection from suffering... The love of God did not protect His own Son...He will not necessarily protect us—not from anything it takes to make us like His Son. A lot of hammering and chiseling and purifying by fire will have to go into the process.
—Elisabeth Elliot

Shortly after my father passed away, Lauren and I found out that she was pregnant with our second child, my fourth child. It was bittersweet news when we found out we would be having the grandson my dad had been hoping for. And it saddened me that he would not get to meet him. I imagine my dad was in heaven grinning from ear to ear as he looked down at his new grandson. Cody was born in December that year, and our family was complete...but not quite.

Lauren and I had vowed in the beginning of our relationship that we would never get married again. We had both been through divorces and were not willing to go down that road a second time. We were living together and had children together, and she even wore a ring. But we had never tied the knot, so basically we were playing house. One day God sent us a message that would convict our hearts to the core.

One Sunday at church, our pastor delivered a sermon about King Solomon and the golden shields. The sermon was titled "The Gold Standard." King Solomon was a man of God and has been considered to be the richest man in the history of the world. After Solomon's death his son took over the kingdom, and things started to change. Here's a description of what happened next:

> Rehoboam son of Solomon was king in Judah. He was forty-one years old when he became king, and he reigned seventeen years in Jerusalem, the city the Lord had chosen out of all the tribes of Israel in which to put his Name. Judah did evil in the eyes of the Lord. By the sins they committed they stirred up his jealous anger more than their fathers had done. They also set up for themselves high places, sacred stones and Asherah poles on every high hill and under every spreading tree. There were even male shrine prostitutes in the land; the people engaged in all the detestable practices of the nations the Lord had driven out before the Israelites.
>
> 1 Kings 14:25–28 "In the fifth year of King Rehoboam, Shishak the king of Egypt attacked Jerusalem. He carried off the treasures of the temple of the Lord and the treasures of the royal palace. He took everything, including all the gold shields Solomon had made. So King Rehoboam made bronze shields to replace them and assigned these to the commanders of the guard on duty at the entrance to the royal palace. Whenever the king went to the Lord's temple, the guards bore the shields, and afterward they returned them to the guardroom."
>
> Following Judah's backsliding, Shishak attacked Israel taking back to Egypt the treasures of the king's palace and the Temple. (This must have been one of the richest plunders of all time since Solomon had been the richest man in all history.) Included in the spoil were

the shields of gold that Solomon had made. These gold shields were in the guard room by the palace, and were held by the guards as they escorted King Solomon to the Temple. They displayed the splendor and glory of their God and the rich blessing He had poured upon Israel. But now they were gone.

What was Rehoboam's response? To cover his embarrassment he made shields of bronze in lieu of the missing golden shields. When Rehoboam went from the palace to the Temple, the same number of guards accompanied him, all carrying large metal shields shining in the sunlight. While at first glance things might have looked unchanged, everyone could see it was the sheen of bronze not the splendor of gold. Imagine the guards who had carried the shields of gold, who had seen the shining display of the glory and blessing of God, and now had to go through the same ceremony with these bronze shields. What a letdown! How embarrassed the people of Jerusalem must have been when they saw the king's procession pretending to have the glory of bygone days.

Like these bronze shields, we have a tendency to polish up our lives to look like gold. We can do this in our relationships at home, at work, and with God. Instead of spending our time polishing up the bronze, we should be getting back the gold.

Upon hearing this message, Lauren and I realized that we had been living the bronze standard in our lives. When we left church that day, we began to plan our wedding, and thirty days later we were married. The message that day was one that not only caused us to look at our relationship from God's viewpoint, but also at many other aspects of our lives as well.

Many exciting things were happening in our lives, and we felt that we were on the right track. Around this time God continued to open many doors in our lives. One of those doors related to my career, and new opportunities began to develop. These new opportunities taught me a new level of experience and growth I had not yet known. Most of my friends and family knew of my sudden job loss and the struggles that I'd gone through afterward. They also knew of the talents and skills that I had and were constantly offering suggestions and opportunities that I should take a look at.

One day I received a phone call from a friend saying he had come across an opportunity that he thought I would be interested in. Reluctantly I decided to go and take a look. It was an opportunity in the network marketing industry. As I sat at the back of the room, I watched person after person walk across the front of the room and give testimonials about the amounts of money they were making with the company. Some of the people were making upward of $10,000 to $20,000 a month. I remember thinking, *if these people can do it, I'm gonna be a millionaire!*

I invested my $500 to join the business, and I fell flat on my face. I had no idea what I was doing. The business model was unlike any business model I had been involved with before. But instead of quitting like most people do in that situation, I dug in and committed to learning everything I could about the industry. I studied the business model front and back. I studied successful people and unsuccessful people in the industry. The thing I loved the most about the network marketing industry was the self-development aspect of it. This was right up my alley. Being in the industry lifted my lid and took me to another level of leadership.

Before long success came my way. I received a company car, I was escalating through the ranks, and I was soon in a position once again where I was speaking, motivating, and inspiring people. It was awesome, and I loved every second of it. I traveled, met new people, and had a lot of fun in the process. But with that success came the temptation of being back in control. I was calling the shots again, and I was in complete control of my own destiny. You're probably thinking to yourself right now, "Man, this guy is a glutton for punishment!" The enemy is very crafty, and if you're not paying close attention, you can easily be led astray.

I began to make choices in my life and in my business that were not in line with my faith. But luckily this time, God spoke to me before I had another epic fail. Some major changes took place within the leadership of the company I was associated with at the time. These changes caused me to step back and take a look at where I was headed with my career and with my life. What was I using my talents and gifts for? I believed I was using them to help others, but was I really? I had spent several years in the industry and had grown a lot from it. I had experienced success, but what was I successful at?

I had yet to be able to reach the success that I had envisioned in my mind. I had read the book *Think and Grow Rich,* and I had studied the industry back and front. I knew that with my talent and experience, I should have been crushing it in the industry. However, I was not getting to that level. I could blame it on the industry itself or the company, and I could also blame it on the leadership or the timing. But I began to realize that the door in that career was not opening and the level that I wanted to reach was not attainable because that was not where I was supposed to be at the time.

Despite the success I had, there was always a feeling inside me that something was missing. There was a void inside of me that I could not explain, and I thirsted for something more. A relationship with God is the only thing that will quench our soul's longing. Jesus Christ said, "I am the bread of life. He who comes to me will never go hungry, and he who believes in me will never be thirsty." Until we come to develop a relationship with God, we are hungry and thirsty in life. We try to "eat" and "drink" all kinds of things to satisfy our hunger and thirst, but yet they remain. Usually when we keep God out, we try to find fulfillment in something other than God, but we can never get enough of that thing. We keep eating or drinking more and more, erroneously thinking that "more" is the answer to the problem, yet we are never ultimately satisfied. This feeling is eventually what caused me to ask that question once and for all.

So I decided to take a step back from the industry and contemplate what I was going to do with my future. But this time, I wasn't going to do it on my own or figure it out on my own. I was going to consult with the one who had guided me through every tough situation in my entire life.

When we are going ninety miles an hour in our lives, it's hard to see and understand what the big picture really is. The only way I truly heard God speak was to just sit back and take a break.

Be still, and know that I am God (Ps. 46:10).

Chapter 8

Purpose Revealed

Purpose Revealed

I told Lauren of my plan to take a break and figure out what God wanted me to do with my life. God blessed me with an amazing wife, who offered her full support during this time. I sat on the back porch of our home for many days praying and listening for God to answer. This was the last time since my father had passed away that I truly asked the question. I asked God what He wanted me to do with what He had given me. I said, "What's the plan? God, if there is one direction you would want me to go in, if there is a purpose that you want me to fulfill, please let me know what that purpose is."

The answer He gave to me was pretty simple. Or was it? The answer was for me to look back at all of the experiences in my life, both the good experiences and the bad experiences. I needed to look back at both my professional experiences and also my personal ones. And in those moments, I would find the clues that would lead me to the answer I was searching for. It's not easy to relive all of your experiences in life, especially the bad ones. I'm sure most people have blocked out a lot of those experiences from their memory bank. And I had done that as well. But the human mind is a powerful thing, and even though I had blocked out some of those moments, they still remained with me.

As I started to pull those memories from deep within, I began to notice a few trends. One of the first major trends I noticed in all of those experiences was that God was present, and that really strengthened my faith. During the good times, it's easy to give credit to God. But to recognize God's work in my life during the bad times was precious.

The second trend I noticed was that no matter what I went through, both personally and professionally, God continued to put me in positions that involved speaking to people. In prison, I was mentoring, inspiring, and speaking to the fellas behind the fence about change. As a national sales trainer in corporate America, I was motivating people to a higher level of performance. And during my time in the network marketing industry, I was inspiring large groups of people to search for something more. No matter what the situation, I was at the front of the room inspiring groups of people to strive for something greater in their lives.

Speaking was something that I had always enjoyed doing. It's been said that public speaking is the number one fear in the world, even greater than the fear of death. Most people would rather have a eulogy read at their own funeral than to give one at someone else's. I, however, was more fearful of not having the chance to speak. Being able to impact people's lives had become something I was extremely passionate about.

Through this time alone with God and this reflection on my past, I began to realize one of the major talents that God had given me. But still I had questions. If speaking did have something to do with my purpose, then where would I start? This time of reflection lasted for a few weeks. I asked God to reveal more; I needed to have more concrete answers to my questions.

About a week or so later, I met with a gentleman I had previously met at a business networking group. Chris was a successful businessman in the community and owned a Christian publication called *Overflow Magazine. Overflow* was in over one hundred churches locally and in many of the local stores and businesses. The magazine consisted of real-life stories from people in the community and how God had worked or was working in their lives. As I sat with Chris over a cup of coffee, I was compelled to share with him my story. What you must know is that prior to telling my story to Chris, the only people who knew of my past were close friends and family.

The enemy had convinced me over the years that if I told people my story, doors would be closed in my face. I was convinced that my story would prevent me from having success in business and in life. I was afraid people would change their opinions of me and look at me differently. I had worked so hard in my life to create a professional image. I had created that image without ever telling my story. I did not know it yet, but telling my story was going to set me free.

When I finished sharing my story with Chris, I felt a sense of relief come over me. But I was still scared. Chris was influential in the community, and I still held the fear that somehow telling him this was going to backfire on me. Instead, God was about to give me more of the confirmation I'd been asking for. After hearing my story, Chris and I connected on a whole different level. Chris is an amazing man of God, and on that day, he became a vessel for God. Chris wanted to put my story in his magazine. *Whoa, horsey,* I thought. It had taken a lot of courage just to tell Chris that story. I felt like I was going out on a limb just sharing it with him. And now he was proposing that I share it with thousands of people in the same community in which I worked?

The cat would be out of the bag and my secret would be public knowledge, and I worried about that. Then Chris said something that I will never forget. Chris said to me, "Steve, God wants you to tell your story." In that exact moment, I knew God was confirming through Chris the answer to my question. And soon my question about how to get started would be revealed as well. In an attempt to be obedient, I decided to share my story with *Overflow Magazine*.

My story launched in the magazine in April 2013, exactly twelve years after my release from prison. I quickly realized what a liar the enemy is. Telling my story had the complete opposite effect on my life than what I had feared. Instead of doors closing, they began to open. It became very clear to me that God was going to use my story for His glory. After the story launched, I began to receive phone calls and e-mails from people wanting me to come speak to their churches, organizations, and businesses. The response brought me to my knees. For the first time in my life, I started to realize what the Lord had been preparing me for all along. The confirmations continued to come. Numerous people came in the days and weeks after to encourage me to become a speaker.

As I began to speak and tell my story in different venues, I was overwhelmed at the response. The Holy Spirit was using my story to change lives. People were being inspired, they were being motivated, and most importantly, they were coming to know Christ.

One of the doors that opened shortly after was with the Fellowship of Christian Athletes (FCA). The FCA is an organization that touches millions of lives...one heart at a time. Since 1954, the FCA has been challenging coaches and athletes on the professional, college, high school, junior high, and youth levels to use the powerful medium of athletics to impact the world for Jesus Christ. FCA focuses on serving local communities by equipping, empowering, and encouraging people to make a difference for Christ.

I was introduced by a mutual friend to the local director of the FCA, Bob Durham. Bob and I met for lunch one day, and he shared with me the vision of the organization and the lives that were being impacted by it. I shared with Bob my story, and upon hearing it, he asked if I would be interested in coming out to one of the high schools to speak to the kids. At this point, I had spoken to many businesses and organizations, but never to a group of teens. I had no idea what to think. But trying to be obedient to what I felt God was calling me to do, I agreed. I thought, *If God wants me to tell my story, then I will tell it anywhere and everywhere that I can.*

When we arrived at Sunlake High School in April 2014, just one year after the launch of my story, we had no idea what to expect. Bob thought we might have around one hundred students, but he wasn't sure. As well over five hundred students poured into that gymnasium, I began to get a little anxious. I prayed that my story would impact at least one life that day. I asked God for strength, and I asked Him to speak through me to deliver His message.

My nervousness subsided, and I took those kids on a journey behind the fence. I shared with them how one split-second decision could impact their lives the way it had mine. I shared with them the harshness of prison life and the seed my grandfather had planted when I was a child. I expressed to them my hopelessness and how God pulled me up off my knees and restored my hope. At the end of the story, I asked them if they wanted to know this Jesus that I spoke of. On that day, we had over 250 high school students accept Jesus Christ as their Lord and Savior.

Sunlake High School was the final confirmation that I needed. What I felt on that day is indescribable. To see God use my story to move in those kids' lives was worth every ounce of pain and heartache I had experienced behind the fence. I knew then what I had been prepared for. I knew that I had been created to inspire people to come to know Him, and I was going to use my story to do it.

"You are a manager of the gifts God has given to you. They may be great or small in your eyes, but they matter to God. 'Now it is required that those who have been given a trust must prove faithful.'" (1 Cor. 4:2).

Why had I not come to realize my purpose sooner? Was it really the enemy holding me back, or was it just my own self-inflicted doubt? Like I said earlier, I believe God won't reveal a person's purpose until he or she is ready for it. The time behind the fence was not enough. It was the culmination of both my experiences behind the fence and the experiences afterward that got me ready. The time had finally come; I had found the answer to life's greatest question. I had found my purpose.

Realizing my purpose and what I was supposed to be doing with my life was invigorating. Understanding that you do have a purpose is exciting and fulfilling, but coming to understand what your purpose is opens up a whole new level of life. Knowing my path lifted a huge weight off of my shoulders and made me feel like I was truly living for the first time. Once I knew my path and what I had been created for, my purpose began to manifest itself. I launched a company called Ability to Influence. Through my years in prison and the years in the business world following my release, I came to realize that our success in business and in life greatly depends on our *ability to influence* others in a positive way. After all, that's what God has called all of us to do.

"'Follow me, and I will make you fishers of men'" (Matt. 4:18–19).

My passion for the kids was not the only passion I had. I was also extremely passionate about helping business professionals and organizations realize the importance of mastering their *ability to influence* others. As a result, I began speaking to companies and organizations on this subject. I had been preparing all of my life for this. My experience in sales and business, combined with my story of overcoming, delivered an effective platform from which to speak. Inspiring people from all walks of life to strive for something greater is what I was prepared for and what I live for.

But it was not until I listened to God that I came to this understanding. When you get good at hearing from God, He's able to use you, and He's able to work through you. And it's through that process that you discover your true purpose in life.

Chapter 9

The Blueprint

The Blueprint

"In him we have obtained an inheritance, having been predestined according to the purpose of him who works all things according to the counsel of his will..." (Eph. 1:11).

Knowing that we have a purpose is important, but how we realize what that purpose is and how to fulfill it are even more important. God laid out a blueprint for me to realize my life's purpose, and He has done the same for you. Moving forward, I want to discuss purpose and the blueprint to find it. I am not an expert on theology; however, I can see how God used every experience in my life to guide me toward my own predestined purpose.

The famous poet and writer Jorge Luis Borges said the following:

"I believe, generally all persons—must think that whatever happens to him or her is a resource. All things have been given to us for a purpose. All that happens to us, including our humiliations, our misfortunes, our embarrassments, all is given to us as raw material, as clay, so that we may shape our art."

Like clay, our lives are molded by God. He lays out our plan like a blueprint. I'm going to lay out the blueprint for you that He used in my life. My hopes in doing so are that maybe, just maybe, you will come to know the purpose God has for your life. Maybe you can plug into the blueprint that I found and realize your path, too. And if you have already found the answer to life's greatest question, then my hope is to inspire you to take your purpose and fulfill it to the next level.

Webster's dictionary defines *purpose* as follows:

"An anticipated outcome that is intended or that guides your planned actions."

An anticipated outcome–what is the anticipated outcome of your life? As I sat in that prison cell at eighteen years old, I began to question this. As I watched the people around me going through the motions of life, I wondered if we really did have an anticipated outcome or if we just existed. I knew in my heart that there had to be more to life. I wanted my life to have meaning, and I wanted my life to have purpose. I anticipated an outcome for my life.

As you read this, what do you see the outcome of your life being? Have you begun to question that, or do you feel as if we just exist? Maybe you are like I was, confused and unsure as to whether there is purpose in life. Maybe, like I was, you're unsure if you alone have a purpose or an anticipated outcome for your life.

Webster's goes on by saying, "An anticipated outcome that is intended..." To me that implies our lives, regarding purpose, are intended for something. But what are we intended for? Not only does your life have an outcome; it also has an intention.

Your life was created on purpose for a purpose. Do you believe that? Have you started to ask the question "What am I intended for?"

The last part of the definition says "...that guides your planned actions." Growing up, I had a plan for my life. I was going to be a football player. I chuckle as I realize how silly I must have looked to God, thinking that I was created for that. What's guiding your planned actions in your life? Is it money or fame? Is it family or friends? Are you living for the things of this world or for something greater? What planned actions are you taking to reach the outcome that you were intended for?

None of my plans have ever worked! When I came to know the Lord, I began to understand that my plans were not in line with the plans that He had. It wasn't until I came to understand His purpose for my life that I started to plan with Him and for Him. This was really the shift that changed the course of my life. The biggest shift was when I realized that it wasn't about me.

> everyone who is called by my name, whom I created for my glory, whom I formed and made (Isa. 43:7).

When you truly start to ask these types of questions in your life, there comes with it a sense of urgency. When you come to the realization that your life does, in fact, have a purpose, you begin to eagerly anticipate fulfilling it. It's almost like it begins to call you.

A few years ago, I heard a story of a wealthy businessman who had been in a severe car accident. This was a gentleman who had reached a high level of success in his life. He had money, recognition, and all of the material things one might want. But as he lay on the ground broken from head to toe and dying, he began to worry. He believed there was a God, and he thought that he was about to meet Him. What scared him the most was thinking that he was about to stand before God and account for the things he had done while he was here. As those thoughts ran through his mind, he realized that he really wouldn't have much to show.

He knew that all of the success and material things he had collected over the years were not going to get him very far. He realized in that moment that he had run out of time. Luckily for him he did not meet God face-to-face on that day. But this event created a shift in his life, and he began to ask that great question. He wanted to fulfill his purpose, because next time he wanted to have something more to show.

When I heard this story, I became overwhelmed with emotion as I asked that same question. What would I have to show if I went today? I wasn't pleased at the time with what I found. It created a sense of urgency within me to figure it out.

Usually it's when catastrophic events take place in our lives that we decide to start asking these questions. For me that event was prison, and for the man in the story, that event was facing death. For others, the event may be the death of a loved one, the loss of a job, or maybe an addiction. But it doesn't have to be that way. We don't have to wait until our world is falling apart to start pursuing our purpose in life.

I'm going to detail the steps in the blueprint that are necessary for you to discover your purpose in life.

1. *Call out to God.*

The first step in the blueprint is to *call out to God*! If you want to find your purpose for existence, why not go to the one who created it?

"'Before I formed you in the womb I knew you, before you were born I set you apart...'" (Jer. 1:5).

Again, you do not have to wait until your life is falling apart to make this decision. But for me, that's how it happened. Remember, as I sat in that prison cell, I felt like I did not want to go on. I felt as if my life were over and I had no purpose. But when I took my granddaddy's advice and called out to God, I came to know that, in fact, my life did have purpose and meaning.

When I speak to kids at schools, I tell them to never underestimate the power in calling out God's name. I tell you the same thing now. I believe if you want to know what your purpose is and how to fulfill it, you must first develop a relationship with God. There is a sense of urgency to this. Like the man in the car accident, we have limited time here. Why wait until tomorrow when you can start realizing your purpose today?

God has given you skills, talents, and experiences for a reason. He has pulled you out of tough times and allowed you to learn valuable lessons from them. Every event in your life has gotten you closer to this moment. Every experience has prepared you for what's to come.

God will reveal your purpose to you when you're ready, but only if you are in communication with Him. When I cried out to Jesus that night in the cell, the communication with Him started immediately. If you want to experience that communication in your life, you have to ask God to take over your life. It's a very simple yet life-changing event. Ask Jesus to come into your heart and ask Him to open your eyes so that you may see. When God opens your eyes, you begin to see things that you never knew were there. They say that hindsight is always twenty-twenty, and this was definitely the case for me. Seeing how God worked in my life ten years after the fact was easy to do, but seeing Him in the moments that events and experiences were happening was not so easy. However, when God opens our eyes, our vision begins to change. This reminds me of the story of the blind man in the Gospel of Mark, chapter 10.

During their travels, Jesus and the disciples were leaving the city of Jericho, and on their way out, an amazing miracle happened...

> Then they came to Jericho. As Jesus and his disciples, together with a large crowd, were leaving the city, a blind man, Bartimaeus (which means "son of Timaeus"), was sitting by the roadside begging.
> When he heard that it was Jesus of Nazareth, he began to shout, "Jesus, Son of David, have mercy on me!"
> Many rebuked him and told him to be quiet, but he shouted all the more, "Son of David, have mercy on me!"
> Jesus stopped and said, "Call him."
> So they called to the blind man, "Cheer up! On your feet! He's calling you."
> Throwing his cloak aside, he jumped to his feet and came to Jesus.
> "What do you want me to do for you?" Jesus asked him.
> The blind man said, "Rabbi, I want to see."

"Go," said Jesus, "your faith has healed you." Immediately he received his sight and followed Jesus along the road (Mark 10:46–52).

As we read this story literally, we see an amazing miracle that took place. But as we look at this scripture metaphorically, we can understand something even more profound. Even though I could literally see, it wasn't until I asked God to open my eyes that I truly began to see life in a different way. Asking God to open our eyes gives us a new understanding of life, and gets us that much closer to realizing why we were created.

Over the years, I have personally seen many people make this decision, and I've witnessed the changes that God has made in their lives. One story that will always stand out in my mind is how God moved in the life of my little cousin Rob.

Rob was the son of my dad's brother Stan. My uncle Stan and aunt Laura had gone through a divorce when Rob was just a little guy. My uncle Stan was a Christian, but not an active one. Church and God were not regular topics of conversation at their dinner table. Rob was an extremely talented kid growing up. He had an arm like a rifle, and he could have easily played baseball or football at a high level. But as he got into his teens, he became very rebellious. He was skipping school, staying out all night, and even doing drugs. Eventually he dropped out of school and had what looked like a bleak future ahead. My uncle was so distraught he even threatened to send Rob into the military, but Rob was still too young for that. Rob looked up to the fact that I was in prison and would even brag to his friends that his big cousin "was doing time."

I had already come to know the Lord at this point and was asked by my uncle to try to talk some sense into him. Rob was much like

I was as a kid; he had his own understanding and his own agenda. My preaching to him went in one ear and out the other. Rob no longer idolized me after all of the Jesus talk that I threw his way. The only option we truly had as a family was to pray for him.

Those prayers were soon answered, and God moved in Rob's life. One of Rob's friends at the time came from a Christian family. On many occasions, she had invited Rob to attend church with them, but he had always declined. Then one day, maybe just to shut her up, he agreed to go to church with her. And what happened to him that day was profound. He had stepped into God's house, and God wasn't going to let him leave the same man. Something happened to Rob in church that day that changed his whole outlook on life. That day my little cousin accepted Jesus Christ as his Lord and Savior.

The change in Rob was much like mine—it was instantaneous. God had changed his heart. Rob went home and flushed his drugs down the toilet. He threw out his old clothes and even began to change his friends. He even told his girlfriend that he could no longer have sex with her. Rob's transformation was extreme; God had truly changed his life.

Since then Rob graduated from Bible college, and he is now in seminary school and raising a family with his loving wife. He has stayed the course and followed the path that God laid out for him. Through his communication with Rob, God revealed to him his purpose. Rob and his story have been an inspiration to me over the years. He is a great example of God's grace and of the power in calling out God's name.

Let the one who created you and your purpose help you to find it. When you make this decision, things will start to change in your life, as they did for me and as they did for Rob. God will reveal things to you that you never knew existed. Doors will open, and God will start to truly work in your life. The communication from Him will come from all different directions, and you will find the path that you should be on. I don't believe I would have found my purpose without taking this first step.

It doesn't end there, however. To develop that relationship and truly let God lead your path, you must come to know Him greater. You do that through prayer and by reading his word.

> "So faith comes from hearing, and hearing through the word of Christ" (Rom. 10:17).

I found that every question I had in life and every situation that I faced could be found in the Bible. It was through the word and through prayer that I truly came to know Christ.

2. Ask the Greatest Question.

The second step in the blueprint is to ask the greatest question you could ever ask: What is the purpose of my life? Don't ask it to yourself. Don't ask it to your friends or family or to your boss at work, and don't ask it to outer space or to the clouds. You have to ask that question to God. It's time to start reaping the benefits of your new relationship with Him.

In their book Soul Shift, Steve DeNeff and David Drury say, "Our problem is not that we seek the counsel of wise friends, follow good leaders, or trust informed voices. It is more that we seek only these things and never learn to hear the voice of God within us."

When I asked the question to God, there was no burning bush that answered me. No angels descended on my back porch to counsel me, and God did not appear in the clouds. The answer came to me from within.

DeNeff and Drury's book goes on to say, "He is calling you out of the white noise of voices you're used to into a silence that is very strange but true. In that silence, God speaks in you."

If you truly believe in Him, then you will believe that He has a purpose for your life. God wants to reveal that purpose to you. He didn't give it to you or create you for it with the intention of you not fulfilling it.

Asking that question will bring you closer to God. Desiring to know your purpose and how to achieve it is pleasing to Him. When I asked that question to Him for the first time, I began to see things happen in my life, and I knew those things were happening for a reason. Even though I did not yet know what my purpose was, I knew that He was getting me ready.

All great and meaningful things in life take time to manifest. This is not a journey that will happen overnight. As God starts to manifest his purpose for your life, there will be ups and downs along the way. Because we are part of this world and in the world, the devil will try at all costs to prevent you from fulfilling God's purpose for your life. And when you truly start to ask the question and to pursue that purpose, the enemy will turn up the heat. Even though the answer does not come to you immediately, stay faithful in your pursuit. Hold faithful to the fact that God will use any and all of your circumstances along the way to continue to prepare you.

Over the course of my journey, I have allowed many things to sidetrack me and take focus away from my pursuit—everything from women in my life to my desire for worldly possessions and success. Stay focused, my friends, as you pursue your purpose. Stay in close communication with God and pay close attention to the choices that you are making in life. Some choices will only delay you from your mission. You must understand that delays, distractions, and disappointments will all be part of your journey. Do not let discouragements along the way keep you from your destiny. And in those moments, don't underestimate the power in calling out His name.

3. *Be Still and Listen.*

The next step in finding the answer to life's greatest question is to be still and listen. Be still and know that He is God. You've called out His name. You've asked Him life's greatest question. And now it's time to listen for your answer. It's time to slow down. Are you running your life, or is your life running you? I was so caught up in being successful that I began to lose myself in the process. More importantly, I began to lose focus in the pursuit of the answer to my question.

I believed God had a greater purpose for my life, and I did not feel that I was living it. I had learned so many great things in the industry I was in. I learned things that took my knowledge of people to a whole new level. I knew that God had used that career as another aspect of my growth process. But I had reached a point where I was starting to sense the void within my life. In order to find my purpose, I needed to slow down and take that break.

When we are going through our lives with blinders on, we can miss out on so much. What are we racing for? Are we on a mission to achieve all of the things that the successful businessman had before his accident? He realized that the things that he had really didn't matter in that moment.

"For what will it profit a man if he gains the whole world and forfeits his soul?" (Matt. 16:26).

Or are we like my parents, who were just trying to survive? Whatever our reason is for going through life at hyperspeed, sometimes we need to just stop, slow down, and listen.

"'Now therefore, o sons, listen to me, for blessed are they who keep My ways. Heed instruction and be wise, and do not neglect it. Blessed is the man who listens to me...'" (Prov. 8:32–34).

When I slowed down and took some time to listen for God, I began to gain a new understanding. This is something we must do prayerfully and then meditate on it. When you take that break and listen for God's answer, you must give your undivided attention to Him. Be attentive!

When we pray, God will hear. And hearing God's clear answers to our petitions is essential. As you spend time with Him through prayer and as you learn to know Him through His word, you will hear His voice; you will learn to view the circumstances of your life with discernment and perceive God's answers to your prayers. God always answers our prayers, but unfortunately, we do not always recognize His answers. That takes practice.

God is not limited to one form of communication, either. He is all-powerful; He is omnipresent; He is sovereign. The Bible is filled with accounts of God speaking to individuals, to families, and to nations. In the past, He spoke in many different ways, and that is true today as well. The answer that came to me during that time with Him was to reflect on my past experiences. In looking back, He revealed to me some very important clues. His answer to me became the next part of the blueprint. What events from your past have shaped you?

4. *Look at the Past.*

The next step in our pursuit of purpose is to look at the clues from our past. I believe those moments will shed some light on your path and on your purpose.

> "And we know that in all things God works for the good of those who love Him, who have been called according to his purpose" (Rom. 8:28).

If we truly believe that God uses all of our situations in life for the greater good according to His purpose, then seeing the good that was created from events in our lives will get us closer to the answer we are seeking. By looking back at certain situations in your life, you can see how God has used them to prepare you.

As I did this, as I looked back at my life, the clues were evident to me. I went as far back as my childhood. The first thing I noticed was how all of the moving around as a kid had prepared me for something later in life. Because my dad was transferred every couple of years with his job, I was forced to make new friends in new places. This benefited me later in life when it came to interacting with others. Being able to make friends quickly made prison life a lot easier for me.

The self-development I learned in prison prepared me greatly for my purpose also. Speaking to the guys in there helped me to develop my speaking skills. My sales experience and training added another level to that calling. And ultimately, my years in network marketing continued my preparation. Even the divorce, the job loss, and losing all of my material possessions built character in me that I would later need to fulfill my purpose. Through all of those experiences, I could see the clues guiding me. I could see that God had been preparing me all along and that He was using those experiences to get me there.

Make a list of events that have taken place in your life as far back as you can remember. Include both personal events and professional events. Don't leave the painful ones out. It's the painful ones that give us the most clues. The painful experiences are really the ones that strengthen us and shape us. They say that everything happens for a reason, and I believe that it does. The reason I was in prison was because of a choice that I had made. God did not put me in prison; I did. But I believe that God used my bad choices for a reason: to prepare me for my life's purpose.

God is not responsible for the choices that we make. But He does use those choices to try to get us back on track and moving in the right direction. God is not responsible for your divorce or for the abuse that you may have experienced at the hands of another person. But God will use those experiences for a reason; He'll use them for good if you open your heart to it. God uses all things for the good of His purpose. Remember, it's not about you; it's about Him.

I've seen many quotes over the years about forgetting the past. Put the past behind you and never look back, and so on. Here are a few examples:

"The only thing a person can ever really do is keep moving forward. Take that big leap forward without hesitation, without once looking back. Simply forget the past and forge toward the future."
—Alyson noel, *The Immortals Series*

"I think the secret to a happy life is a selective memory. Remember what you are most grateful for and quickly forget what you're not."
—Richard Paul Evans, *Grace*

"Life is short as breathing!
Forget yesterday, Focus today to enjoy tomorrow!
The purpose of life is to live it."
—Ebelsain Villegas

"For some, excavating the past isn't an adventure, it's more akin to tearing a Band-Aid off an open wound."
—Raquel Cepeda, *Bird of Paradise: How I Became Latina*

The list goes on and on...I could write a whole book with quotes about forgetting the past. But I'm not, because I tend to disagree with this advice. Don't get me wrong; I'm not telling you to dwell painfully on past experiences to the point that it causes you to crawl into a hole never to return. But what I am telling you is that your life story, both the good and the bad, makes up your testimony. And your testimony is going to play a major role in finding and fulfilling your purpose.

5. *Look for the Messages.*

After I asked the question and slowed down to take the time to listen, confirmations about the answer I was receiving came from all different directions. Many times God will use people and circumstances to answer your questions. The time I had spent alone with God had truly refreshed me, and I was excited and nervous about the answer I had received. I'm a hardheaded individual. I needed some more clues; I needed some more confirmation. All too often, we lean unto our own understanding of things. We doubt ourselves, we doubt our futures, and at times, we even doubt the answers that God gives us.

But He knows that. For us hardheaded people, He will continue to bring the answers until we get them through our thick skulls. That's what He had to do with me! It was obvious to me that God was sending people to me; it was too coincidental. When Mr. Pass told me in prison that he had a feeling that I was going to go and do great things, it was confirmation of exactly what God had told me in the cell a few nights before.

After I sat on my back porch for weeks alone with God, Chris with Overflow told me that God wanted me to tell my story. I was connected with Bob and FCA by a mutual friend named Jim. Bob wanted me to tell my story. Then person after person encouraged me openly to become a professional speaker. Even this book was encouraged by many people sent to me by God. Was it coincidence? I think not. God was answering my question and guiding my direction.

Sometimes it is easier to hear a message through another person. God may ask someone to tell you something. That person may not know what the communication means, but he or she will feel a strong desire to deliver the message. God won't force the person to do so, but He will be persistent. Only God knows the why behind the communication, and the other person doesn't have to know why to deliver the message. As you open your eyes and your ears like you have asked God to help you do, you will begin to notice His communication coming to you from many different people and places.

A good friend of mine named Joe Jackson received a calling from God to plant a church in Wesley Chapel, Florida. Sounds like a great location, but Joe lived in Indiana with his wife and three children. Joe knew no one in Florida. Was God really calling him and his family to do this—calling them to move thousands of miles away from all of their family and friends to start something new?

One night Joe had a dream that he didn't understand. He dreamed he had a third daughter named Savanna. The next day they were visiting a church and met a cute little girl in the children's ministry named Savanna. Weird, he thought. After church they went to their favorite restaurant, where they were served by a waitress who just happened to be named Savanna. Was God trying to tell Joe something? Sometime later, while driving through town, he noticed that the car in front of him had a custom license plate that read "SAVANNA." All of this happened over a period of two days' time.

The clues and messages were coming. And though Joe was recognizing a common message, he still was unsure what it meant.

"For God speaks in one way, and in two, though man does not perceive it" (Job 33:14).

Upon researching the area, Joe realized that the town of Wesley Chapel was a natural savanna. They traveled to Wesley Chapel to pray for discernment. Was God really calling them there? Was this place the message he had been receiving all along? When bad directions landed them in a remote area of Wesley Chapel, they found themselves sitting on a ten-thousand-acre savanna. Joe knew he had received his answer. In that moment, a new church in Wesley Chapel, Florida, was born. It would be called Savanna Church.

6. *Take a Leap of Faith.*

The next step in the blueprint is to put the wheels in motion and take that leap of faith. After asking God to take over my life many years before, I started to ask the question: What is my purpose? I then had to be still and listen to God's response. Part of His answer was to look back at my life experiences. In looking back, I found many clues but still needed some confirmation. So I paid close attention to the messages that He was sending me. Once I had received my answer, I needed to do like Pastor Joe did: I needed to take some action.

Once Joe received his confirmation, he moved his family one thousand miles and started Savanna Church from scratch. Joe got started with the faith that God was going to show him the way. I took that same leap of faith when I walked away from my career and started Ability to Influence. Finally understanding my purpose was exhilarating, and I wanted to get started immediately.

"I hope you live a life you're proud of. If you find that you're not, I hope you have the courage to start all over again."
—Eric Roth

Finding God's purpose for your life does not mean you will have to drop everything else in your life and start over. Sometimes it will, but not always. Whatever God has created you for will find its way into your life if you're searching for it.

"Ask and it shall be given you; seek, and ye shall find; knock, and it shall be opened unto you..." (Matt. 7:7–8).

Connecting with and living your purpose is an awesome journey that typically unfolds in mysterious and surprising ways. It's not something that can be forced; God will always reveal your purpose to you when the time is right. I like to think of it as a treasure hunt; it's a perfectly paced adventure, with your eyes and heart wide open.

Maybe you're like I was in the cell that night; you don't believe you have a purpose, and you feel like maybe life has no meaning. Not believing that you have a purpose won't prevent you from discovering it, just as a lack of belief in gravity won't prevent you from falling. All that a lack of belief will do is just make the process take longer.

Here's a story about Bruce Lee that puts this idea in perspective. A master martial artist asked Lee to teach him everything he knew about martial arts. Lee held up two cups, both filled with liquid. "The first cup," said Lee, "represents all of your knowledge about martial arts. The second cup represents all of my knowledge about martial arts. If you want to fill your cup with my knowledge, then you must first empty your cup of knowledge."

If you want to discover your true purpose in life, you must first empty your mind of all the false purposes that you've been taught (including the idea that you may have no purpose at all). Empty your cup of understanding, and allow God to fill it with His.

When you are ready to take that leap of faith but are scared out of your mind, here are some words of wisdom that I have learned along the way. I hope they support you in taking your own path with joyful courage.

1. Listen to the voice in your heart.

God has some very important things to say to you along the way. Make sure you always stay in tune with Him. In a society where we tend to look to outsiders for advice, we tend to ignore our inner voice. When you have a gut instinct about something, trust it and follow it. Remember, He will guide you.

2. Take care of yourself.

When we take the road less traveled, it can be stressful, which is why it's so important to stop, breathe, and nourish your body and soul in whatever way works for you. Go for long walks, or sit on the beach and stare at the ocean for a while. Whatever calms you and relaxes you, do it.

3. Replace your fear of the future with excitement for what's to come and the joy that comes from living out your purpose.

Being in the unknown can be scary, but try to replace your fear with a desire for the passion you are pursuing! Take five to ten minutes every day and visualize this desire. What does it look like? What does it feel like? Who is around you? Think about the lives that are being influenced in a positive way by your purpose.

4. Develop relationships with like-minded people.

Search out people who are also living on purpose. Surround yourself with people who are encouraging and supportive and share the same values and beliefs as you. Want to do good things and be successful at doing so? Hang out with people who are doing good things successfully.

5. Don't compare yourself to other people.

It's easy to get wrapped up in time lines and to compare yourself to what your peers have already cultivated. Everyone has his or her own respective journey of what he or she is manifesting in life. Focus on your relationship with God, and trust that if you pay attention to what He says, your journey will happen exactly as it's supposed to.

6. Celebrate what has happened so far.

I equate the pursuit of one's passion to a treasure hunt. The path is never clearly laid out, but we get clues along the way that give us assurance that we're not out of our minds for pursuing it. Celebrate your clues, and celebrate what you cultivate along the way; use the clues as reminders to not give up when the end result isn't happening as quickly as you may want it to.

7. Remember, you are awesome because God is with you.

Remember that you are love, you are joy, and you are awesome. No matter what others say and no matter what roadblocks you encounter along the way, God is with you. Be patient, stay focused, and hold onto how abundant God's purpose for your life is, and eventually, everything you need will come to you.

Chapter 10

Common Purpose

Common Purpose

As we follow the blueprint of our lives searching for each of our individual purposes, we must come to know that we all have a shared purpose as well. As brothers and sisters in Christ and as brothers and sisters in life, I believe that we share a common responsibility and a common mission while we are here. You see, our life stories are the smaller stories that make up God's story. He created the heavens and the earth, and that was just the beginning of His story.

We tend to get so caught up in our own lives and our own stories that we forget we were created by Him for Him. Growing up I never knew that I was part of His story, so much so that I would play a part in it. When I asked God to come into my heart on that prison floor, I realized for the first time that I was important to Him and to His story.

In coming to know Him, I began to understand how my testimony played a part in that story. I realized that my mission was to share that testimony in order to bring people to know the bigger picture. Every aspect of my life has given me the opportunity to connect with and witness to others. Those experiences, from the good to the bad, all give an aspect to the story that someone can relate to. God equips you throughout your story to help you share His. This is a purpose that we all share, and it's called "The Great Commission."

After Jesus Christ's death on the cross, He was buried and was resurrected on the third day. Before He ascended into heaven, He appeared to His disciples in Galilee and gave them these instructions:

> Then, Jesus came to them and said, "All authority in heaven and on earth has been given to me. Therefore go and make disciples of all nations, baptizing them in the name of the Father and of the Son and of the Holy Spirit, and teaching them to obey everything I have commanded you. And surely I am with you always, to the very end of the age" (Matt. 28:18–20).

What does this mean for us? It means we better get started! Jesus told us here what He wants us to do. He's called us all to a great responsibility and to share in that mission. He has called us all to tell His story to the world.

> "But you are a chosen people, a royal priesthood, a holy nation, God's special possession, that you may declare the praises of Him who called you out of darkness into his wonderful light" (1 Pet. 2:9).

A good friend of mine named Rachel Moodie is sharing in that mission. Rachel was a bubbly and outgoing twenty-four-year-old with a smile that would light up the room. She and her husband, Matt, had just bought their first car and their first home. They were excited about the future and full of life. They were newlyweds in love and on top of the world. But only nine months into their new life together, they realized something one day that changed their lives forever.

One day Matt noticed a lump on one of Rachel's breasts. After noticing it Matt encouraged Rachel to have it checked out. Rachel wasn't worried and told Matt that she would have it checked at her next appointment, which was only a few months away. Feeling inside that something was wrong, Matt insisted she not wait. At her appointment the doctor did not believe the lump was anything to worry about, either, but decided to send her for tests just to be sure. The results of the tests showed that Rachel had stage-two cancer.

Shocked and scared, Rachel held tightly to her faith. As a believer she knew that somehow, in some way, her story was going to be part of God's story. Rachel underwent seventeen weeks of grueling chemotherapy, followed by a double mastectomy and reconstructive surgery, all at the age of twenty-four. During the two weeks between hearing the news and starting treatment, her tumor more than doubled in size. If she had waited the few months for her scheduled appointment, she may not have been with us today. Throughout it all, she maintained her bubbly attitude and her smile that continued to light up a room. She became the patient who lifted the hopes of all the rest in the hospital. Rachel took every opportunity to tell the other suffering patients about God's story. And in doing so, she brought some hope to the hopeless.

She continues sharing in our common purpose today by giving her testimony to women from all walks of life. She visits Moffitt Cancer Center regularly, sharing God's story with the women currently fighting the disease. She continues to volunteer with the American Cancer Society and their Making Strides against Breast Cancer program. And as a director with Mary Kay, she continues to empower women everywhere with her story.

God recently added another miracle to Rachel's story. Rachel and Matt had always dreamed of being parents one day. Prior to starting her chemotherapy, Rachel had been sharp enough to do her research. Realizing from her research that the chemo treatments could prevent her from having children, she consulted a fertility specialist prior to starting her treatments. Before starting her chemotherapy, Rachel had five embryos frozen and kept safe from harm. Recently Rachel gave birth to a beautiful little girl, and that little girl has become another miracle to add to Rachel's already amazing story. Rachel's individual purpose continues to contribute to the common purpose that we all share.

I have come to understand over time that the purpose we all share is a privilege. Having the opportunity to impact other people's lives is truly a gift. And it's a gift that has eternal significance. We live in a short-term culture and tend to value the temporary things in life. In coming to understand our purpose, we begin to understand its long-term importance.

A man who knows that eternal significance well is Jim Willis. Jim is a successful businessman with a passion for discipleship. It's been said that there is no one better on a mission field than Jim, and he has been a great friend and mentor to me over the past few years. His story is a true testament to how God's love guides us in our common purpose.

As a child, Jim's homelife was volatile, to say the least. Physical and mental abuses were a daily occurrence at the Willis house. When Jim was thirteen, his parents went through a bitter divorce. Jim began drinking and staying out all night, and sometimes he stayed gone for the entire weekend. After two years, he was going downhill academically and socially at a very fast rate; he had not seen his dad since the divorce. His mother added no relief for the pain that he was experiencing. One night he made the mistake of being home when she arrived from work. As she walked by, she did that parental second look, stopped in her tracks, and said, "You look just like your father, and I can't stand to look at you anymore. I want you to leave and never come back! In fact, I never want to see you again."

So at fifteen years old, Jim became homeless, helpless, unloved, and unwanted. Living in a tree fort that he built in the woods, Jim managed to keep himself in school. He even got a few jobs and fully supported himself. Eventually he got out of the woods and into an apartment in a single-adult community. However, living in a singles complex came with many opportunities to party, and Jim became consumed by that party lifestyle. Even though Jim was out of the woods quite literally, he was more lost than ever.

One day Jim ran into an old friend whom he had not seen in years. Steven and Jim had done everything together growing up. They were partners in crime and the best of friends. Much like Marks and I, they had been inseparable growing up. After catching up Steven asked Jim to catch a movie with him. When they arrived at the theater, Jim knew he was in the presence of Christians. He could tell by their cheesy grins from ear to ear. Jim was mad at Steven because he knew that he'd been tricked.

Even though he was infuriated with Steven, Jim went inside anyway. As he sat there contemplating an escape route out of the theater, a preacher named Billy Graham came on the screen. Mr. Graham said something that night that would change Jim's life. He said in the midst of evangelizing that "Jesus loves you." And for the first time in life, at the age of twenty-three, Jim heard that someone actually loved him. Overwhelmed and excited by the news, he was ready to give his life to Christ. Jim said, "Come on, Steven. Let's go down together!" After all, they had always done everything together as kids. But Steven was already saved, and that night was about giving a lost friend the same opportunity.

Jim dropped to his knees amid the popcorn, candy wrappers, and spilled soda to ask God to take over his life. He describes the joy and peace he felt that night as "something sent down from heaven." Today Jim takes every opportunity available to give his testimony to others. Over the years God revealed to Jim his individual purpose in life, but even more important, He revealed the purpose that we all share. Jim knows his story is part of God's bigger story, and he tells it with the same love and compassion that God gave to him.

We could fill a million books with stories about people fulfilling God's purpose for their lives. But we could also fill a million books with stories of people who have not yet found their purpose. We have to remember that it's not called "The Great Suggestion"; it's called "The Great Commission," and we have all been called to it. Like I said earlier, God communicated to me that night in my prison cell that there were two forces pursuing me. Both forces have purposes they look to accomplish with your life. You can decide not to choose either side, but either way, you are still helping one of those forces accomplish its goal.

It's pretty deep when you really stop and think about it. God has an overall purpose for your life that complements and glorifies His story. And the devil has an overall purpose for your life, too, that complements and solidifies his. Your life and your purpose will become part of one of those stories. It's inevitable, and there is no neutral territory and no common ground to stand on. Satan will tell us that being a good person is good enough. He will convince us that even if we don't believe in Jesus, that's OK, because our good deeds can get us into heaven. When we believe that, we are fulfilling his purpose. We don't have to be mean or evil people to please the enemy.

We are all witnessing examples of this in the United States right now. As the powers that be remove God from our government and our schools in the name of fairness and equality, they are helping to fulfill a purpose. Those powers that be might be great people with caring hearts. They may live their lives with good morals and ethics. They may donate to charities and nonprofits, and they may even follow the Golden Rule in their lives. However, the story they are telling is not God's story. And as they play a role in removing God's story, they are helping to fulfill a purpose that we know is not from God. At some point in our lives, we will have to draw a line in the sand and decide whose purpose we will share.

"God did not create evil. Just as darkness is the absence of light, evil is the absence of God."
—ALBERT EINSTEIN

The Testimony

The best way for us to share in our common purpose is through our testimonies. I say it all the time: our success in business, in life, and in fulfilling our purpose is greatly dependent upon our ability to influence other people in a positive way. I'm so passionate about this idea that I decided to name my speaking and coaching business Ability to Influence.

The most powerful tool that you have when it comes to influencing people in a positive way is your life message. It's also one of the most powerful tools that God gives you to utilize in sharing His story. Your life message is really made up of four parts.

The first part is your testimony. Who are you and why? Second are your life lessons. Talk about your successes and your failures and how they impacted your life and how you have grown from them. This is crucial when connecting with people. People will find things in your life lessons that they can relate to. Third is to talk about your passions. Discuss your passions in life and how they relate to your relationship with God. And last but not least, tell people of the good news. Tell them about God's story and your purpose as it relates to His story.

As I began to share my testimony and my life message with people, it was amazing how they began to open up. People found things in my story that they could relate to, and the doors would open. It was also amazing to me just how many people were lost and searching.

So how do you share your testimony? You can easily revert back to the stories in this book for some guidance and examples.

What was it like before?
The first thing you want to do is tell what your life was like before you asked God to take it over. Remember, not all

testimonies are as dramatic as the ones you have read about in this book. Your testimony can be just as powerful to others even if you have not experienced tragic events in your life. Everyone has gone through something that people can relate to. It can be something as simple as a void that you felt in your heart prior to knowing the Lord.

How did you come to realize?
The second thing you need to do is tell others how and when you realized that you needed Jesus. What was going on in your life at the time to bring you to that realization? Be descriptive here and don't hold back. Don't sugarcoat the situation and don't be scared of judgment. Put it all on the table for them; otherwise they will hold back, too.

How did you do it?
Thirdly, you need to tell others how you committed your life to Jesus. Where were you? What was the atmosphere like, and what did you say to God in that moment?

What's it been like since?
Lastly, explain the difference God has made in your life. What has happened to you since you gave your life to Christ? How have you seen God move in your life? If you have come to realize your life's purpose since then, share that with them as well.

Your testimony, no matter how weak or strong you feel it is, has the power to change people's lives. And God wants to do just that with it. Understand that you matter significantly. I hope that hearing my story and the others in this book has sparked something inside of you. I hope that you have started or will start asking that great question for yourself. If you've already received your answer, I hope from Prison to Purpose inspires you to keep pushing forward and to stay focused. It's not always an easy road, but nothing of value is ever easy to achieve, especially when it has eternal significance. One of my favorite quotes when playing football and still today is this:

> *"I firmly believe that any man's finest hour, the greatest fulfillment of all that he holds dear, is that moment when he has worked his heart out in a good cause and lies exhausted on the field of battle—victorious."*
>
> —VINCE LOMBARDI

Recently I returned to my high school alma mater after twenty years. I stood on the same field where I used to play ball so many years ago, and I delivered my testimony to the school's football team. That day a large number of the players accepted Christ as their Lord and Savior, and many more rededicated their lives. It was a full-circle moment for me that I will never forget. As I stood on that field, I was reminded of just how far God has brought my life. In that moment, I felt victorious.

Remember that as the battle rages on for our lives, you do play a part even if you don't play. Sitting on the sidelines still has a massive impact on the outcome of your life. Get in the game and never give up. Don't stop searching for the answer to life's greatest question. Hopefully the blueprint God used in my life will help you along the way, and I pray that God blesses you for allowing me to share my story with you. I am excited for you, I'm excited for your life, and I'm excited to share in our common purpose with you.

Two final thoughts—never stop pursuing the answer to life's greatest question, and I will tell you the same thing that a wise man told me many years ago: "Never underestimate the power in calling out His name!"

Bible Verses

Chapter 2

Hebrews 3:10

Chapter 4

Proverbs 11:2

Chapter 5

John 1:5, Luke 1:79, Ezekiel 11:19, Jeremiah 29:11

Chapter 6

Isaiah 55:6–7, John 14:13–14

Chapter 7

1 Kings 14:25–28, Psalm 46:10\

Chapter 8

1 Corinthians 4:2, Matthew 4:18–19

Chapter 9

Ephesians 1:11, Isaiah 43:7, Jeremiah 1:5, Mark 10:46–52, Romans 10:17, Matthew 16:26, Proverbs 8:32–34, Romans 8:28, Job 33:14, Matthew 7:7–8

Chapter 10

Matthew 28:18–20, 1 Peter 2:9

Works Referenced

Clestine Herbert–The Purpose Coach
http://www.DivineDiscipline.com

Joe Jackson–Savanna Church
http://www.savannachurch.com

Rachel Moodie
http://www.marykay.com/RMOODIE

Rob Hopper

Chris Cherp
http://www.overflowmag.com

Jim Willis
http://thewillisagency.com/

Steve DeNeff / David Drury
Soulshift: the measure of a life transformed
Copyright 2011, 2012
Published by Wesleyan Publishing House
Indianapolis, Indiana
ISBN: 978-0-89827-599-5

All quotes from
http://www.goodreads.com/quotes/

For additional influential self-development tools from Steve Hopper, visit http://www.AbilitytoInfluence.com.

Additional Materials from Ability to Influence

The Colors of Influence

We are all a combination of each of the four personality types; however, there is always one type dominant in each of us.

As you strive to learn and master the ability to influence others, understanding the different personality types is imperative to your growth.

Imagine walking into an event, and upon meeting someone for the first time, you know almost right away what will trip his or her trigger. I mean that in a good way. What if you knew that person's strengths and weaknesses, but most importantly, how to influence him or her to action?

That is what you are going to receive from this amazing training! Let's have some fun, and let's master the Ability to Influence!

THE
PRODUCT
THEY REALLY WANT
IS YOU!
IT ALWAYS HAS BEEN.
AND IT ALWAYS WILL BE YOU.
STEVE HOPPER